More Than Hope

More Than Hope

A Guide to Interventions

For Families and Friends of

Addicts and Alcoholics

Steve Bruno

Foreword by Allan Sosin M.D.

www.SteveBruno.com

For Janna, a true friend

And in memory of Baxter, my best friend

Foreword

I have known Steve for many years and, from what I have observed, he not only maintains high professional standards but is also quite knowledgeable and effective in his work.

I am fortunate enough to work in the same profession, where our focus is on helping people out of some of the darkest situations one could imagine, and addiction is right up there when it comes to dark and seemingly impossible situations.

According to the National Institute of Drug Abuse, over 10% of the United States population suffers from acute drug addiction or alcoholism. Of these 33 million Americans, only 10% receives treatment. As a nation and as a planet, I am certain we can do better, and being able to do an effective intervention is an important first step in this direction for many of us.

Having been Medical Director for several detox programs, I appreciate the importance of a well-done intervention. Many of my clients would never have arrived safely were it not for Steve and other professionals like him.

The drug epidemic we face today is not going to simply go away. It requires the ability to face the problem and some knowledge of what to do about it. I know from first-hand experience that families are looking for answers, and the questions they are asking are not easy to address, especially when it comes to doing something like an intervention.

In fact, one of the hardest things to do when it comes to addiction is to be able to face it and then do something about it. That's why this book is so important.

It is our job to help our loved ones realize that survival is possible and that life can be enhanced without drugs.

This applies not only to illegal and legal "recreational" drugs but to all drugs that affect the mind. Using a chemical substance to modify thought interferes with the individual's ability to create his own reality.

When you take the power of drugs away, you must give something back, or the individual will feel diminished. That is the purpose of rehabilitation: to rejuvenate the individual's capacities and help him restore abilities he has lost.

These changes permit the individual to see the future as an opportunity instead of as a struggle; to see other people as friends instead of as adversaries and to see himself as the creator, not the victim, of life or his environment. Once he achieves this level of responsibility, he will naturally abandon the need for drugs.

Human beings possess enormous capacities for positive change.

This book can help you get the person you love to a program where he can achieve these things and–hopefully–move on to live a happier life.

My advice is to take what you are about to read to heart. If you do, you won't have to depend on luck *nearly* as much.

Allan Sosin, M.D.

www.iprogressivemed.com

Acknowledgments

I'd like to further express appreciation to Dr. Sosin who, in addition to writing the Foreword for this book, has been my longtime friend and occasional physician, and to his wife Susan; to Tom Paquette, President of The Foundation for a Drug Free World, for encouraging me no matter what; to my entire family, especially my parents Betty Ann and Russ; to my good friend and skilled technical writer Janna Trevisanut; to Cathy Caccavella; to Gail Ford and Sonja Schluter for their editing prowess, and to my best friend Baxter for helping, unwittingly, both my clients and me in so many of my cases.

I would also like to acknowledge all parents, grandparents, siblings, offspring, spouses, co-workers and friends who are determined to help someone they love.

Table of Contents

Part IV. My *Exploding* Workshop (Six Case Studies)

Introduction

If drugs or alcohol were an addict's fundamental problem, recovery would be a walk in the park.

The fact is that addiction is a set of conditions that cut across many aspects of an individual's life, which becomes more and more degraded as he turns to self-medication as a solution. Excessive drinking and drug use in turn worsen his situation, leading to the illusion that they are the cause of his problems.

The real demon, however, is not what is in the bottle, the baggy, the needle, or the pipe. If it were, anyone who could detox could stop using or drinking permanently. But ask anyone like me, who's been down that road–that isn't what happens.

I wish every family could understand what it's like to be an addict because seeing things from that viewpoint can help you create solutions for the addict in your life. That's why I wrote this book. As a professional interventionist, my most powerful tool is my ability to see things from the addict's point of view.

I don't try to scare addicts out of using or drinking by citing statistics about how life-threatening it is, or how he might end up in jail. If you've tried this approach, you know these kinds of warnings fall on deaf ears.

When I facilitate an intervention, I look at it as a real-life game, but I don't see the addict as my opponent. When I see an addict, I see someone in a prison, and it's that prison I'm playing against.

The fact that the addict's life is in my hands motivates me to challenge and outmaneuver the mechanisms that are shackling him.

How does one win a game of Texas Hold 'Em? By knowing when to bluff, fold or play. How does one win in an intervention? The same way—by thinking ahead several moves at a time and keeping your eyes on the prize.

The prospect of doing an intervention is intimidating, and effective tactics are not always easy to come up with. Mulling over what *might* happen can be enough to make you want to curl up in a ball and stay in bed, and, not only because of your fears about what the addict might do, but because of how the family might or might not pull together.

Even if you get your loved one to go to treatment, what will happen once he's there? If he's in denial, is it a waste of money? Is it selfish not to try? Will your life be in greater ruins *because* of the intervention? These questions plague families and cause them to remain paralyzed.

Excuses for putting off doing an intervention are easy to come up with: doctors' appointments, court dates, weddings, vacations and everything in between. Ironically, the same thing is happening to the addict. If he were to go to a good program, he could get his life back in order and be happy again, if only he would just get up, pack his stuff and *start*. But he has a list of things he must do before treatment can even be considered. This cycle of promises, efforts and failures on the part of the addict *and* his family can continue for years.

Families get results when they stop finding reasons to wait. Ninety-nine percent of the time it's best to get a program in place and to start mapping out the intervention *immediately. Move things forward.*

Get a program in place and start mapping out your intervention *now.*

In terms of the big picture, effective treatment is key, an intervention leading to a program you feel has the best possible chance of returning your loved one to a balanced and controlled state, able to face the challenges and experience the joys of life once again.

If a person can confront his unhappy circumstances, repair the damage of his past and regain his sense of responsibility and identity in an organized and supportive atmosphere, then he *can* discard drugs or alcohol as a solution.

Dependency on drugs or alcohol doesn't happen overnight; it evolves. Along the way a person's internal compass gets buried; north begins to point south, west only leads to a desert, and the addict acts in ways that go against his own values in a desperate hope of finding a new oasis. The way back becomes more and more difficult. Guilt, shame, anger and regret meld together into a blackness that consumes the individual. At a certain point, drugs and alcohol bring only fleeting relief from this massive and ongoing emotional conflict.

As the addict's betrayals, deceptions, and crimes weigh down on him, he begins to exhibit hostility, aggression, isolation, manic behavior, including bouts of deep depression, no longer able to operate as he was meant to. Add to this the pressure he may feel from family, from work, from the expectations of himself and others—now a long list of failures and disappointments—and you have someone in very bad shape who will remain that way until the mess is cleaned up. He has lost his way.

Although they may tell you otherwise, addicts are not happy people. When I used drugs and drank, I had happy times, but in truth, the more I used, the emptier I felt and overall, the more depressed I became.

No matter what the drug–when I took it, bought it, prepared it or used it–I knew what I was doing was inherently wrong but that didn't stop me. I preferred to believe it wasn't as bad as my family made it out to be, that I could control it and that the obstacles I faced were somehow not my fault (or were *all* my fault).

I would ruminate, "If people would only *believe in me*," or, "I just need this one thing paid for." But getting clean was something I put off because I was sure that my being stoned wasn't the problem. The way I looked at it, getting high made my problems bearable.

I had no idea *what* was wrong with me, but I believed if I only had a different job or my rent paid, I could regain my footing and live the way I knew I could and should. I would think, "Right after this bag of meth, this bottle of vodka, this bag of pot, *that's* when I'm going to get my life together." But, that day never came: This is the cage most addicts and alcoholics live in.

Families sometimes think the solution is to move their loved one a thousand miles away. Invariably however, his problems follow. Prison inmates, for example, are sometimes clean for years and yet, once freed, they return to their addictions. This is because the underlying reasons for the addiction are not actually confronted or repaired, so the condition continues.

Over time, the addict or alcoholic becomes further conflicted with himself and retreats more and more into the comfort of a chemical embrace. He begins to perceive himself as a victim, blaming others for his problems. At a certain point, the drugs or alcohol are merely a retreat from the worst of it and, while they may soften an addict's perception of his decline, at the same time they worsen it. Ironically, the self-serving addict ends up with less and less until he has nothing left at all, another example of why addiction is a prison, a black hole which evolves beyond his control, a rip-tide drowning him.

Luckily, many addicts have loving families who reject our invitations for self-annihilation and seek ways to rescue us instead.

The real solution is to get the person back to being his true self again, unburdened from his past transgressions and able to make decisions based on conscience with the potential to live a purposeful life. The fact that you are reading this shows that you believe it can be done. And you're right, *it can.*

A good intervention is simply the first step, albeit an important one.

While helpful guidelines exist, no formula fits every situation. Even after reading every book on the subject, including this one, you won't have every answer you need. My hope is to instill in you a sense of navigation so that when unique situations arise you can face them effectively.

I can point you in the right direction, but the story of *your* intervention is a path you must walk yourself. In any case, I hope you find perspective here, learn to have patience and how best to take action and, most of all, to persevere.

Families often ask me, "What if we fail?" But the better question is, *"What if you succeed?"*

More Than Hope

Part I

My Unexpected Journey

From Addict to Interventionist

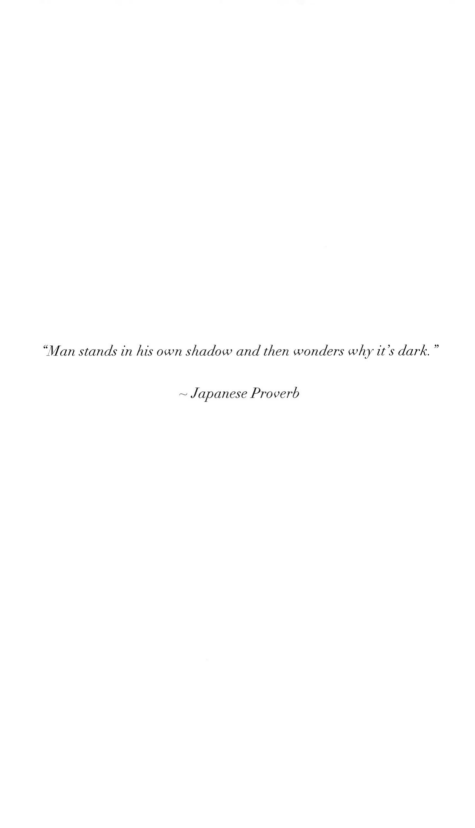

"Man stands in his own shadow and then wonders why it's dark."

~ Japanese Proverb

One Foot in The Grave, The Other on a Banana Peel

(My Life as an Addict)

*G*rowing up, I was more interested in what my two older brothers and their friends were doing than being around other kids my age. Being able to hang out with two popular, teenage Alpha males was like having a backstage pass to adolescence.

Like a lot of kids with divorced parents, I lived with my mom and saw my dad once or twice a week. Without fully understanding why my father had left in the first place, my young mind placed me at the center of the universe, and I concluded that it must have been my fault.

Well-intended as both of my parents were, they were not present during the hours I was *supposed* to be in school. We had a live-in maid but she never assumed to try to raise us, so I was mostly left to learn about life from my brothers and their friends. To them, though, I was a tag-a-long, a wannabe.

One of the activities I tagged along to was watching my brothers and their friends smoke pot, act like clowns and get the munchies. *Of course* I wanted to be part of it. Eventually, during what I imagine was an after-school get together (or after *cutting* school), someone in that group handed me my first joint.

What smoking pot did for me was like nothing I'd experienced. Problems at school, trying to fit in with older brothers, divorce–all of it melted away with every inhale of the thick, sweet smoke, and an inner door opened wider and wider to a place where I was surrounded by a cushion of carefree happiness. It was my own, private freedom.

Needless to say, I *loved* getting high.

I grew up in the 70's. My brothers were doing what many teenage kids their age were doing in that decade: experimenting with pot, cutting school, and occasionally eating mushrooms or dropping acid. By the time I was eleven, I had experimented with all these things and habitually used tobacco and pot.

By the time I was twelve, getting high had become routine. At this point, the drugs and alcohol were causing side effects like fatigue, poor concentration, and memory loss. My grades plummeted. By the first semester of 7th grade, I was failing completely.

There weren't a lot of recovery programs for twelve-year-olds. Not knowing what else to do, and with a financial boost from my grandmother, my mother enrolled me in a well-respected boarding school in Calistoga, California. I went from cutting school and smoking pot on a daily basis to living in a controlled, residential environment where buying drugs was simply not an option. There, attending small classes with one-on-one attention, I graduated with straight A's.

The following year I went back to public school, close to where I grew up in Oakland, California. I soon gravitated to a group of students who were more interested in getting high than in getting to class. It wasn't long before I began to smoke pot again. Eventually that included a list of other drugs. This led to my becoming even more isolated and depressed. I barely made it through ninth grade.

My mother intervened again and placed me in a local, private school where I managed to pass tenth grade.

When I was 17, I started forging my parents' checks to get money for cocaine; I can still recall sitting in the study downstairs in the house where I played as a child, staring out the window with one of my mom's checks in my hand, trying to figure out why I was betraying the people I loved, and who loved me. On impulse, I decided I'd move to Hawaii and become a waiter on a cruise ship, far, far away from check forging and hurting my family. It seemed like an idiot-proof and romantic solution to my problems.

I remember waiting at a union hall on Oahu living on muffins from a convenience store until they called my name. I spent about a month working aboard the U.S.S. Constitution before I gravitated to the other waiters on the ship who *also* liked to smoke coke. I ended up losing my job. Shortly after, I moved back in with my father in Oakland and enrolled in a local community college. Another *new start.*

I stayed in a small camper trailer in my father's backyard, believing, if I could just get back to being a good student, my problems would go away, but my problem wasn't a lack of school or a job. My problem was that I had lost my way. I had developed so many bad habits, one of which was to be blind to my bad habits, so they crept up on me just when I thought I'd broken free.

Up to this point, my substance abuse had been limited to smoking pot, snorting or smoking cocaine, drinking and the occasional LSD trip. But my résumé was about to change: crystal meth would take its toll on my body, mind, and spirit–as well as my family's–for the next decade and a half.

It began when an unsavory character moved into the house near my dad's. His girlfriend and daughter both lived with him. When I walked by him polishing his motorcycle in his driveway, we said hello. He told me he was a Hells Angels' "prospect," someone the biker gang was considering for membership. I had no way of knowing if this was true and no particular desire to find out. The next time I saw him, he invited me over for a beer and we hung out in his garage. Eventually, he took out a bag of tiny white crystals. He had a smile on his face as he looked at me and looked back at it, as if he knew a secret. I watched him intently.

He put some of the crystals in a spoon and added a little water. Then he took out a syringe and crushed the mixture with the flat end. I leaned forward and watched as he pulled back the plunger and filled the syringe with the faintly yellowish liquid. I felt like I should have been afraid but I wasn't. Instead, I was excited to watch him shoot up.

He took off his belt and wrapped it around his bicep. Then he flexed his fist, which made the veins in his arm bulge out. I looked away for a moment and turned back just in time to see the liquid disappear into his arm.

He changed in front of my eyes: from looking relatively normal to suddenly having a resplendent grin stretched across his entire face; the whites of his eyes grew bigger and brighter by the second. He set the needle down, pulled the belt from his arm and let out an enthusiastic snort. I watched him dance around the garage for a few minutes, accentuated by an occasional full-body shiver. Then, without a word between us, it was my turn.

His motivation? As a kid with access to money and willing to get high on just about anything, I was the perfect mark.

He was creating a customer.

I didn't need much convincing; my life was boring and this was *obviously* going to fix that.

I watched as he set the syringe up again just like he had the first time. As he pushed the plunger again, this time with the needle in my arm, my entire body *filled* with what felt like pure adrenaline. Every cell in my body started vibrating at high frequency. My vision became sharper. It was like someone poured rocket fuel directly into my brain and lit it on fire. My mind raced. Thoughts clamored. I couldn't remember standing but I found myself pacing around the garage. I felt *incredible*.

Two days later, not having slept, I was upstairs at his house with one of my friends from school. We were hanging out with him and his girlfriend. I saw a baggy of the same crystals peeking out from under a fold in the bedspread. When no one was looking, I took the bag and put it in my pocket. I made an excuse and exited down the stairs and through the garage. On my way out, I picked up one of the syringes from his workbench.

When I got back to my trailer I took the bag out and looked at it. The tiny crystals glistened in the dim light. I poured quite a bit into a spoon and mixed in the water like he had. As I crushed the crystals, the water turned pale yellow. I pulled up what I thought was a good amount into the syringe, much more than before, and slid the needle easily into the throbbing vein just beneath my skin. I pushed the plunger in.

That was the last thing I remember.

I woke up the next day in the exact spot where I had shot up, only I was lying on the floor, too dehydrated and too weak to move.

The phone was mounted on the wall above me. I knocked the receiver down with my foot and dialed my mom.

I barely managed to stand. I walked outside and down the driveway along the side of my father's house. My mother had just arrived and was walking toward me. She was looking at me intensely. As I got closer I could see tears on her cheeks.

I remember looking at my face in the car visor mirror. My skin was clammy and gray. It was artificial looking and shiny. My eyes looked recessed and had *really* dark circles beneath them. I looked like I had been made up as a zombie for Halloween.

My mother cried as she drove me to Gladman Hospital in Oakland. Listening to the *thwick, thwick, thwick* of the pavement beneath the wheels, one question persisted in my mind: What had *happened* to me? Reflections floated on the glass at strange angles as I stared out the window; everything seemed to be moving at different speeds, just like how I felt, disoriented, like I didn't know where I was. I *was* a brilliant, beautiful young man who was going to conquer life, *wasn't I?* The man I saw in the visor mirror was neither; he was as stupid and ugly as a person could be, and headed for disaster.

At the hospital, I did the first of what would, over the next 15 years, grow into a list of residential programs ranging in length from one to six months. When I was finished, my family and I agreed that relocating would be a good idea, but soon I learned that moving away, even with a new job, wasn't enough to solve an addiction.

I moved to Reno to live with my brother. When my addiction continued there, I moved to upstate New York to go to the most prestigious culinary school in the world where, after just a few months, I was arrested on campus for possession.

Shortly after that, I did a 30-day program in Queens, and relapsed the day I graduated. Then I moved to Manhattan and landed a kitchen management position, hopeful I could stay clean and finally have some normalcy in my life. This chapter would, however, duplicate the last several. I ended up smoking crack along the outskirts of Central Park, eventually losing my job, my room and living in a cardboard box.

After a few weeks of spiraling toward oblivion, my father bought me a bus ticket back to Oakland. After a five-day bus ride to get away from the wreckage of my addiction, I bought some crack from one of my old connections before I'd even unpacked.

At one point, what I regard as my all-time low, I sold my stepbrother's great-grandfather's *very* valuable violin for $15 so I could buy *just one more* bag.

I had become the *worst* kind of person I could imagine. I was a thief, a drug addict, a liar and a traitor.

Again on impulse I decided to move to New Orleans, a place completely new, imagining I'd sip whiskey, learn the Delta Blues and sing about my suffering.

I almost lost my life–again–shortly after moving there. I had found my way into the notorious Ninth Ward where a guy tried to sell me a piece of a peanut instead of crack. I ran. He chased me. Six blocks later, after I thought he'd given up, I bent over to catch my breath and instead found him standing right behind me. He kicked me hard, square across my face. I remember falling to the ground, the wadded up $10 bill still clenched in my fist. He grabbed my hair and started smashing the back of my head into the concrete, trying to pry my fingers apart, but I hung on tightly to the dirty, wadded up bill, clenching my fist tighter. Someone had been watching all of this unfold and called 9-1-1.

As an ambulance pulled up, the guy left me in a pool of my own blood. The $10 bill was still in my fist. That's all I cared about.

As I stared into the black and starless sky, unable to move my head, my arm aching from clenching my fist–but feeling oddly victorious–I saw a wavering, orange glow that cackled occasionally. A car was engulfed in fire a few hundred feet from where I lay. I could feel the blood pooling around my head and beginning to soak into my shirt. It felt almost cool. I thought that was odd, *it should feel warmer.* A paramedic leaned over me just as I faded to black.

When I came to, I was unable to move. My neck had been braced and I was strapped tight on a gurney. My shirt was gone. They had cut my pants in the ambulance. I was on a stretcher being wheeled into the brightly lit lobby of a hospital. The EMT guys paused for a few minutes. I looked up at the bottom of their chins as they surveyed the overcrowded lobby, positioned the gurney along a wall in the hallway, and left me there strapped to it.

I was *dying* of thirst. After a few minutes, I unclamped the brace from my neck, rolled myself off the gurney and started searching for a drinking fountain. As I approached the information desk the security guard looked up, stood up, and reached for his gun. I froze. Was someone standing *behind* me? It took me a moment to realize that the emergency room had fallen silent. Everyone was looking at me. I turned and found myself looking at a stainless-steel panel on a pillar. There was a man staring back at me from the wavy, heavily scratched reflection. His hair was matted and he was splattered head to toe with dried blood. For a minute I wasn't sure who–*or what*–I was looking at. He had no shirt, both pants legs were cut or torn.

One of his shoes was missing.

Several days of stubble on his cheeks and neck put him in the category of either being homeless, crazy, or both. For a few seconds, I was confused. *Was that me?* I waved my hand. The man waved back.

I began to laugh.

I laughed because, even in this utterly dilapidated state, all I could think about was getting out of there so I could go back with my ten dollars and get some coke!

People kept on staring. I kept on laughing.

At times, I've felt like putting a bullet in my head. I would think, "I'll disappoint everyone all at once. Get it over with. They'll grieve, sure, but at least I'll stop hurting them. Better they have the memory of me than the presence of me stealing, hurting and lying all the time." I fantasized about my family and friends lamenting my loss at my funeral. They would finally see that I wasn't selfish at all; they would see that I loved them so much I was willing to *kill myself* in order to stop hurting them. I could never bring myself to shop for a gun, though. Believe it or not, my spiritual convictions prevented me from ever carrying it out.

I wanted out, but when my family would offer help, I told them things weren't as bad as they thought, that I could make it on my own. I got angry and indignant, but part of me kept thinking I should take them up on their offer; maybe getting away for a while was a good idea. Just…not *today.*

Maybe tomorrow. Or Monday. Monday is *always* a good day for a new start…

Any day but *today.*

My Intervention

"You can't run from trouble. There ain't no place that far."

~ Uncle Remus

The thing I remember most about that week is feeling like the world was closing in on me.

Less than a year earlier, I was a manager at Eurochow, a restaurant owned by the famous Michael Chow. We catered to Hollywood's A-List elite. I even had an office that overlooked the Armani Gallery off Rodeo Drive. In the week of this story, however, I was working part-time, selling classified ads for a flea market newspaper. My primary activity, and the reason for my recent, rapid decline, was my rekindled love affair with crystal meth.

I was staying with my girlfriend in her three-bedroom townhouse. We shared it with her mother–*and* her mother's 35 cats. And, whatever you can imagine conditions that that number of cats in a confined space could create, imagine it ten times worse and you begin to get the picture.

In addition to smoking meth as often as I could, I was drinking about a quart of vodka a day, smoking a lot of pot, and intermittently taking the anti-depressants Paxil and Wellbutrin.

I was also working in a small factory where we made bongs as well as the meth I was using. My boss and dealer Rosanne (Rosy) occasionally fed everyone, cooking rice and sausages in dented pots and pans on an electric hot plate in the garage. Those meals were few and far between but, with all the meth everyone was smoking, *who the hell was hungry?*

17

I had been looking for a treatment program for months. Low to no cost programs are typically not very appealing, and they tend to have long waiting lists. My mother had been calling me regularly, hoping I would find one and go.

At one point, she called and asked if I would meet with her and a counselor. She said she was driving down from San Rafael and wanted to meet in Malibu.

The prospect of going to Malibu was appealing. I'd only seen it on TV. Besides, my parents would be more inclined to continue doling out money if I showed that I was earnest and wanted to improve things in my life. And, in many ways, this was true so I agreed to the meeting.

That week, my girlfriend, her mom *and* her mom's 35 cats were evicted from the townhouse. I came home to find a deputy sheriff standing on the doorstep with a locksmith changing the locks. He gave me 20 minutes to get my stuff and leave, so I rushed upstairs and grabbed what few possessions I had at the time: my "Tangerine" iMac (remember those?), some clothes and my 6' Nile Monitor lizard, Cyn (a Welsh word meaning *kin*).

I had nowhere to go. I called my mom and made my case; she agreed to pay for a hotel for a few days as long as I made it to the counseling appointment.

I figured it had to lead to something better than what I was dealing with so I started focusing on possible ways to exploit the situation. I suspected though that, regardless what I might plan, the meeting with my mom and the "counselor" was likely to be an intervention.

On the day of the meeting my brother Mike came by to pick me up.

I may have been paranoid but I wasn't stupid; I told him I was going to drive my own car. I wasn't sure what the result of the meeting was intended to be. My worst fear was that certain members of my family might try to have me committed. In any case, I set out for Malibu on my own.

After an hour or so, I arrived at a wooded area that opened to an expanse of buildings that looked like one of those recovery programs advertised on TV. It was all white and looked like a little palace.

Gravel crunched beneath my feet as I approached the main entrance.

There was an enormous tray of pastries on a table in the foyer, as if someone was expecting a large group. Without introducing myself, I asked the guy standing in the foyer if I could have a croissant. He smiled, nodded, walked over to shake my hand and told me his name was Will. He motioned for me to sit down in one of the overstuffed chairs arranged in a small alcove off to one side. I couldn't imagine people who were being committed getting either croissants or big puffy chairs, so that was a good sign.

He spoke to me for a few minutes, telling me about his own experiences with drugs and treatment. *Wow,* I thought, *just dump your purse out.*

I helped myself to another croissant while I listened to Will's confessions. Eventually, he seemed satisfied that he had created a bridge of common ground between us or whatever it was he was doing and then he guided me into a room where I found my family, seated and waiting.

My father was there, which surprised me. I hadn't seen him in a few months, not because of any particular animosity between us but because of the simple fact that, when my life was falling apart, he tended to distance himself from me, undoubtedly a healthier stance than most parents usually take. My brothers were also there, my stepfather and my mom.

They all seemed very solemn. *Maybe I died,* I thought, *and this is my funeral, and Will is the Ghost of Crystal Meth Past, showing me the people in my life whom I'd wronged.*

But—no such luck.

They each held a piece of paper. Some were handwritten, some were wrinkled, others neatly typed. I found out later that these were the letters that Will had told them to write. After an awkward couple of minutes, he motioned for my father to read his aloud. One by one, my family read their letters to me. Occasionally, someone would become emotional. Mom cried. I responded to something that started my brother and stepfather arguing. I remember my brother Dan yelling at me, then at Mom, then at me again. I remember my brother Mike and his calm demeanor not registering with me. He stayed quiet except for his letter which, like the others, was a carefully constructed plea for me to accept help (whatever *that* meant).

It seemed like no one in the room felt any more confident than I did. This made me feel better. They were trying to do *something* for me, so I tried to relax and waited for the letters to be over.

My brother Dan explained that he knew about a program that was different from the ones I had gone to before; this was the help my family was asking me to accept.

I could give a *crap* about "different therapies." I had tried them all, hadn't I? Now, my family was asking me to go to treatment *again.*

This would be the sixth or seventh residential program—to say nothing of all the outpatient and by-appointment therapy I had been through over the years. Honestly, I could not fathom how they had come this far with me *intact*. Was *I* the crazy one in this scenario, or were *they*? It's not that I wanted them to go away; I just couldn't understand what they were still doing there. Yet there they were, some reading their letter with sincerity tinged with sadness, others obviously under orders, but this was my family, here to help, for better or worse.

I understood what the basic offer was. Mom and Dad were ready to write another check for however much (I immediately saw this as their future loss since I was certain I'd screw this up if I did go). I would have to tuck my tail between my legs, ashamed of the way I was trying to solve my emotional problems and walk through the doors of some institutional building and say hello to people I didn't know. I imagined them scrubbed clean, shiny, starched creases; bright, fluorescent lights; someone handing me a clipboard with a stack of forms to fill out and a pen with the facility name imprinted on it. I had a sudden fear of not knowing what I would write: *Loser. Failure. Just shoot me.*

I felt suddenly that I shouldn't go. *It won't end well* I thought. I have done this before, *voluntarily*. It has *never* ended well. *Then again*, I thought, *neither is anything I'm doing now.*

I didn't know *what* to do. I was out of alternatives. My girlfriend Alice had moved into a one bedroom along with her mom and the 35 cats. There was no room for me, not that living with 35 cats in a one-bedroom apartment would have been particularly appealing.

I asked what would happen to Cyn and the two kittens I'd rescued from Alice's mom. At this, my father's conservative demeanor cracked, "Good grief! Are you serious? You need to get *rid* of those animals."

I felt indignant but said nothing. Get *rid* of..? What does *that* mean?

Will tried to mediate. I'd forgotten he was even there. He invited me outside to have a cigarette. We stepped out into the cool air of the inner courtyard. We talked for a few minutes, puffing on our smokes. Then out of nowhere he walked over to me and gave me an unsolicited hug. He said, "I love you, man."

I remember thinking, *Get the f**k away from me, Dude.*

I decided right then I would handle things on my own.

I went inside and told everyone that I would think about it. Then I went outside and got into my car, telling those who came out with me, "I'm not going right now. I have a place to stay for another week. I'll think about it," declining my mother's teary-eyed invitation to dinner.

I was coming down and starting to feel that familiar, gentle panic in my gut. I needed to get some shards (meth) into my system. I didn't care about anything else except filling a glass pipe and watching the crystals melt into a puddle as I sucked in the smoke in an effort to fill the huge, gaping hole in my life.

Ironically, it was my dealer who prompted me to go.

When I told Rosy about the intervention, she looked at me thoughtfully for a few long moments through the wisps of meth smoke in the little room in the back of the bong factory and calmly said, "Steve, you should go."

I looked at her, a little stunned. She continued, "Look, David and I have actually been really worried about you. Look at how much meth you smoke. You drink way too much. You are high all the time; you look like shit and you keep coming back for more. *Go.* It sounds great. If I could, *I* would go."

There was genuine sorrow in her eyes. I felt a sudden pang of guilt; she wasn't my mom or dad. She was my dealer, but I knew in that moment that I was going to treatment. As if in response to my silent visualization, she got up and said, decisively, "I'll set you up for your trip."

She gave me about an eighth of an ounce of meth. With that and a glass pipe, I gathered up my stuff, crammed it all into garbage bags, grabbed the handle of my computer, collected my lizard and the two kittens from Alice's cattery, piled everything into my semi-dilapidated, 1971 MGB GT, and hit the road.

That was on a Tuesday. I proceeded to smoke meth, drink beer, smoke pot (and about a carton of cigarettes) over the course of a 300-mile drive that took until the following Sunday to complete.

On the last day, I was driving on Highway 5, just past the Highway 33 junction when my tire blew. I pulled off the road and found myself alone, the flat expanse of the San Joaquin Valley, an endless, dusty horizon in all directions. On one side of the highway was a turnip field, on the other an onion field, and in front of me, a guy looking down at me lazily while the tractor upon which he sat rattled, sputtering occasionally as if to urge him along.

I had a 6' lizard sunbathing next to me and my 1971 MG, and one kitten had made a beeline into the onion field. I found her before she had gotten too far. The situation was compounded by the fact that I did not have a phone. I was stuck. I attempted to explain my situation to the guy on the tractor. He had no idea what I was saying but remained unapologetically intrigued by what he was seeing.

Eventually, I flagged down a car. The driver allowed me to use his phone.

Vaguely, I remembered I belonged to AAA and, by some miracle, managed to dig my membership card out from beneath the pile of flotsam on the floor of my car. I called a tow truck, thanked the driver for the use of his phone and sat down with my menagerie to await rescue.

After a while, a big flatbed arrived. Once my car was loaded on the truck bed, he informed me that I had five free miles. "Where do you want to go?"

What? I could *see* five miles in every direction–those vast turnip, onion and dust fields I mentioned. On top of this was the fact that it was Sunday afternoon.

"Everything is closed," he told me. I had a blown-out tube-type tire which most repair shops aren't equipped to fix anyway. I had no idea what to do. "What are you *trying* to do?" He asked, taking a mild interest in whatever my backstory might be.

"I'm far from home or anyone I know. I'm a meth addict. I'm trying to get to a treatment center in Santa Cruz. I don't know what to do."

He surveyed me silently for a few moments while his truck idled in the background, then said, "Give me a minute." He hopped into the truck. I could see him talking to someone on his phone, but I couldn't make out what he was saying. After a few minutes, he walked back over to me. "Get in the truck," he said, "I've got a buddy who'll open his shop and fix your tire for you."

On the way, he told me that he, too had been a meth addict for about ten years and that his family had sent him to treatment. He was rescuing a fellow addict–no denying that. He seemed happy with himself.

24

He drove me *35 miles* to a little town where his friend was standing in front of his shop, smoking a cigarette.

We called my brother Mike who paid for the tire. My MG went up on the rack. The owner made the repair and put it back on my car. He rolled it out of the shop and said, "Do well in treatment," as he smiled and handed me the keys. Before I knew it, I was back on the highway.

Part of me felt like that had all been a sign from God, but another part of me knew that I still had meth left. Both parts were happy. I drove into the night, smoking and drinking until I ran out of everything.

I rolled up to the treatment center around 2:00 a.m. with my lizard, my cats and computer in tow, two empty cans of beer in the cup holders and three garbage bags full of my stuff crammed in the back.

The staff had no idea I was going to show up. I still feel bad for the woman on watch that night. Here I came, stoned out of my mind, sputtering and rattling up the otherwise silent country road in the dead of night in a beat-up MG occupied by a tiny zoo of animals, a week of beard on my face, then digging through everything I owned.

I apologized for my appearance as I started rifling through my car, looking for god-knows-what beneath the silent, star-filled sky. I remember she just looked at me as I narrated a short history of various items I came across in my car, and kept telling me I should probably go to bed.

The next morning I sat down with the admissions counselor and told her matter-of-factly, "I have nowhere to go, no other options, but I am not going to look for answers in the same ditch I have looked in before. If this is going to be just a bunch of group therapy and psych drugs, I'm leaving."

She looked at me, unmoved and said, "There's none of that here.

We have a whole different approach. You should think about staying for a little bit. See what you think."

At that moment, the program director walked by. He had overheard the conversation and said, "Come to my office." I went in and sat down in a chair that looked comfortable but wasn't. He sat cross-legged on top of his desk, looking down on me with a big smile on his face. *This is weird,* I thought.

"I completely get where you're coming from," he said. "Our purpose is to help you to get back to your life. We don't want you to stay if you don't want to be here. We can at least help you with the first step, which is withdrawal."

A few awkward moments passed. "If there is no place for my lizard and my cats, I am definitely not staying."

The director held up both hands as if to say, "I get it," called in the woman I'd spoken with earlier and explained my position.

She went away to make phone calls while I sat with my cats in her empty office. About an hour later, she came back and said, "Okay, your brother is going to take care of–*Cyn*, is it? He has a friend who can build her a habitat. Your mother will take care of the cats until you have completed the program." With that handled, I agreed to stay. Shortly after, I started the paperwork, then a staff member came into the office and calmly asked, "Excuse me, but why is there an *alligator* in my office?"

I was in withdrawal for about ten days. They brought me food, took me on walks and let me sleep (and sleep).

The program was holistic and did not follow the notion that replacement drugs are a good idea, which in most cases I agree with.

Five and half months later I graduated in the best shape I've ever been in. Two weeks after *that* I was hired to do my first intervention and two days after *that*, I got my first client into treatment.

As much as I fought the intervention and my family, as much as the thought of treatment depressed me, as much as I felt victimized and resisted the entire effort to get me into treatment, once I was through–once I was done–to this day I cannot think of a proper way to truly thank my family for what they did. If my family hadn't done the intervention, I never would have started doing interventions for the hundreds of families I have helped since then. I certainly never would have written this book.

Think about that as you move forward, about the moment in *your* future when the person you love, who is now fighting you, comes to you and says, *"Thank you."*

Mom's Version

by Betty Ann Bruno

"It's not easy being a mother. If it were, fathers would do it."

~ Bea Arthur

For our family, the hardest part of Steve's intervention was convincing ourselves that sending him to yet another drug treatment program was going to be different this time. We had been around that block before, for more than 20 years. Each time Steve entered a treatment center, our hopes would rise, and then, after a year or two, gradually ooze away as we helplessly watched our youngest son relapse into drug and alcohol abuse and lose everything all over again.

This time, Steve was 32 and approaching the bottom of another slide. The pattern was familiar to everyone. The first sign was that he stopped going to AA meetings. He made the excuse, again, as he had at other times, that he was doing well, didn't need the meetings or was too busy with his job. Then, he began taking an occasional glass of wine, or a beer, followed by harder drugs. He lost his job, then asked for financial help, all the while denying he was relapsing. In the family, we would mention our concern to each other but none of us felt we could do anything except watch, and mourn. The pattern was repeating again. Valuable things began to go missing, there were more lost jobs, each one a rung farther down the ladder. Then Steve was evicted from his apartment, in danger of being on the streets again, or...worse. Well, if you're reading this book, you already know what happened.

It had been about a year since the slide began. He was working in a factory that made bongs and other drug paraphernalia. He tried to convince the family that he wasn't using and we wanted so hard to believe that. We were grasping for anything to cling to that might save him from drowning in the swamp of drug abuse. Later, Steve told me that his employer was actually paying him in drugs. Isn't that great? Your employer is your supplier! Well, he couldn't pay his rent with the "wages" from the bong factory, so he lost the rooms he had been renting and went to live with his girlfriend, Alice, her mother, and her mother's 35 cats.

He still had a car, but it barely ran. I gave him money to have some repairs made so he would be safer on the road and then he made a request which may sound both strange yet familiar to you:

"Mom," he asked, "If you will contribute $100, I can buy the materials to make play stations and litter boxes for Alice's mom's cats. She's been good to me and I'd like to do something nice for her in return. How about helping? I can build everything. Actually, I've already started because Dan gave me some money. Think you could do that?"

I wanted to scream. "Why don't you just take care of yourself!! How can you even *think* about taking care of somebody else's cats when *you* are in such bad shape?"

But, I didn't. Logic had little to do with Steve's thought processes at that point. And he got very defensive whenever anybody in the family criticized him. So instead I said, "Okay. I'll chip in. But you know the real solution is to get *rid* of those cats. There's no way to keep 35 cats in a small house."

He was using god-knows-what drugs. His own life was in chaos, but amid that chaos he was trying to bring some order into someone else's life. So messed up, I thought. So sweet, but so messed up. It was extremely sad.

30

When Steve needed medical attention, I told him I was glad to pay for it to encourage him to make and keep appointments, which mostly he didn't. I was trying not to enable him, but the line is blurry. It's much easier to profess your belief in Tough Love than it is to practice it on a day-to-day basis. I don't like to think about that time, but I have to in order to write this. As I look back on it, I can't help but ask myself: What could I have done differently? What *should* I have done?

As the days passed, my heart ached for what I couldn't do for my youngest son. I liked getting phone calls from him because if he was on the other end of the line, at least I knew he was still alive. But I also dreaded hearing from him because every phone call was such a charade; neither one of us could speak the truth. He was such a con, telling us things were going to be better if we would just ... (fill in the blank). I kept on a smiley face, trying to find ways in which I could be supportive without being a total "co." We both pretended everything was normal.

Sure, it was perfectly normal to have 35 cats urinating and defecating in your house. It was perfectly normal to keep busy taking care of those cats because you couldn't hold down a paying job.

Speaking of normalcy, I was about to have a major birthday, a tough milestone and *I* needed help. I didn't want a *big* party. You know, with a guest for each year of my life, or anything like that. I just wanted to be with my husband and three sons for a few days in a place everyone would enjoy. The problem was that any family gathering would have the same old problems we always had when Steve was using. There was no place we could run to escape that sad reality.

Ultimately, I decided that I wanted the time with my whole family more than I didn't want the negative aspects that would come with Steve being with us. I decided on Ashland, Oregon, home of The Oregon Shakespeare Festival, which had been an annual event for me for many years. My husband Craig loved going there too, but none of the boys had ever been so it seemed like a good choice. They all said they wanted to do it, even Steve, so I rented a vacation home in Ashland for a week and ordered a fistful of tickets to the plays.

Steve's brother Mike also lived in Los Angeles and offered to pick Steve up and bring him to Oregon. That was comforting. Mike was extremely dependable and, if he said he would bring Steve, then that meant Steve would be there. I very much wanted all three of my sons to be with Craig and me. That's the way I pictured it happening. That's what I really wanted. I waited for my birthday week with heavily guarded optimism.

I had something to give to the boys on my birthday. I had been working on it for several months. I was going to present each of them with a book of stories I had been writing for them, stories of my growing up, stories of my father, whom they had never met, stories of other strong and interesting characters who had helped shape my life, stories I loved to tell and thought my sons would someday like to have, illustrated with pictures from the family album.

I indulged in daydreams about presenting the books of stories: It would happen as we lingered over breakfast coffee. I would make a little speech about the stories and tell them how proud I was to give each of them a copy of my book. Then all three of them would stay at the table, pour over the stories, read each other passages. It would be a magical morning of sharing memories. I loved playing out that reel and its variations in the days before my birthday week began.

Of course, nothing in real life ever meets your fantasies, does it?

Craig and I arrived at the house in Ashland the day before the boys were scheduled to get there. He and I took the downstairs bedroom and left the two bedrooms and bath upstairs for the boys to share.

We used our first day to settle in, filling the cupboards with groceries for breakfasts and snacks for late afternoons and nights after the plays. I wanted the week to be super-special. Dinners would be in Ashland's wonderful restaurants. Every day we would see at least one play. I also bought tickets to the backstage tour so the boys could see how one of the country's outstanding repertory theaters creates its production magic.

Mike and Steve arrived first and pulled into the driveway alongside the house. Mike bounded up the steps first. He looked great, as usual, but as my gaze moved past him to Steve, I covered my mouth with my hand to muffle a gasp. Steve looked terrible, ill and unkempt. His eyes were dull, his face covered with a few days' stubble, his shirt tail hung out, his shoes were torn and his sockless feet were filthy.

"Steven, what's wrong? You're limping!"

"Oh, I've got a sore on my foot. It'll be okay," he assured me as he gave me a lifeless hug.

When he let us examine his foot, we saw an open and infected sore. After some nagging, he finally consented to soak his foot in hot salt water to cleanse the wound, but he showed little concern about it. Another bad sign.

He browsed the cupboards, founds the makings for a sandwich and, saying he was really tired, went to his room.

As Steve's footsteps retreated up the stairs, Mike turned and said in a low voice:

"He slept all the way up here. Wasn't a bit of company. Had nothing to say. Just slept. And, I'm not sharing a room with him. He's gross. Dan and I can take turns with the bed and the floor in the other bedroom. Neither one of us wants to bunk with Steve. Just give him a bedroom. Nobody else even has to go in there."

My birthday week was not off to a great start.

For the next few days, each of us took on the roles we had played before: Steve would wake up sometimes and join the rest of us at a play or at a meal, but most of the time he slept. In fact, he was in withdrawal, although the rest of us either didn't know it or didn't know what to do about it. I pressed on, trying to have as good a time as I could, but inside…I was crying. Mike, who has always been the most successful in not letting Steve get to him, explored the quaint theater town and tended to some work he had brought with him. Dan tried to keep Steve in the normal family routine. He made frequent trips to Steve's room to get him up in time to get to a play or to dinner. But not even Dan was able to keep Steve in the family loop all the time. He still missed one play, the backstage tour and one lunch, maybe a dinner. I don't remember. I just know that somehow we managed to enjoy ourselves and have some good moments despite a deep, dark hole of hurt in the midst of our group.

"What I know is that he needs to go to treatment," I would confide to anybody who would listen. I said it aloud as much for my own benefit as for the other person. I was trying to convince myself there was something that could help him, that he wasn't hopeless. But, nobody wanted to listen anymore. I'm not sure I believed it myself. We were all exhausted from living with an addict for more than two decades; we were all tired of being ripped off, tired of being manipulated.

"What good it is going to do?" "And who's going to pay for it?" "Can you afford it?" "What about when the treatment program is over?" "Where's he going to live?" "How's he going to support himself?" "What have we not tried?"

I didn't want to obsess over it or let it take us over during our vacation week but, whenever Steve wasn't physically present, I found myself returning to the same questions and not finding the answers.

I handed out my book of stories and everybody flipped through the pages, but no one spent any real time with them. I kept my disappointment at bay by telling myself that the boys would read the stories after they got back to their own homes.

Dan and Craig organized a wonderful gift to me from all of them. Dan put in the money for Steve's share so he could sign the card, too.

The week finally ended. We said our goodbyes with fixed smiles, our eyes focused just behind each other's heads. The pain in my heart was more clearly defined and sharper than it had been six days earlier. As soon as we got back to the Bay Area, I picked up the phone to begin working on getting Steve back into treatment. The first person I called was Steve's dad. His response was less than enthusiastic:

"Well, where's he going to go? Where's the money coming from to pay for it? I sure don't have it. He owes me quite a bit already, not that I ever expect to see it again. I wish you good luck, but I can't help. He'll just f**k things up again anyway. Spending money on him is just like putting it down a big rat hole!"

My husband Craig reacted the same way.

"You've already spent tens of thousands of dollars on Steve, and it hasn't gotten him anywhere. As far as I'm concerned, for all the money and other things he has stolen from me over the years, I don't care what he does with his life anymore. It's his to throw away if that's what he wants to do with it, and he seems determined to do exactly that. He's had more opportunities than ten other people and has thrown everything away. I'm out of patience."

Steve had obviously used up all his goodwill and burned some major bridges. There wasn't a lot of sympathy left in the family.

Then, Dan called. I hadn't realized it, but he'd also gotten on the phone as soon as he'd returned home.

"Mom, I've got a couple of leads on facilities for Steve. Either one might work. You can look them up on the internet or just call them. Want the numbers?"

Mike, too, was looking. His best friend was a counselor in the Los Angeles area and had suggested the place Steve had been in two years earlier. They were exploring the possibility of Steve returning there. I felt good knowing that I wasn't alone in the effort. Still, it wasn't easy. It's difficult to find a place in which you have confidence and that you can also afford. The right treatment center is a subjective and personal choice, for you and your addict. You both have to feel good about the place and the people who work there. Usually all you have to go on is a website, a brochure, and a voice on the phone. There isn't time or money to visit all the places personally and look into the eyes of the staff or the addicts in residence. It's just one more difficult task in the life of an addict's family.

I wasn't having much luck. The program Steve had graduated from most recently was full and did not encourage returnees. A hospital program he had been in a few years earlier had changed focus. Other programs had long waiting lists or didn't seem to be quite right. One program was for adolescents, another for ex-felons. Steve was a user, but he wasn't a felon. The thought of his living with hardened ex-criminals did not appeal to me. He was still my sweet son who, even in a drug haze, wanted to help a dotty old lady take care of her too-many cats.

My years as a news reporter came in very handy. I could conduct fairly thorough interviews on the phone and wasn't afraid to ask questions. Experience had taught me the difference between honest answers and BS.

After a couple days of intense searching, we decided on a facility we felt held promise. Money for treatment would have to come out of my inheritance from my mother which I had earmarked as a legacy for my sons. I knew that Dan and Mike might resent my spending thousands more dollars on Steve, so I cleared the matter with them. We agreed Steve's treatment would come from his share of the inheritance. They wouldn't be penalized; it wasn't going to come out of their pockets.

That was the practical aspect. Dissipating the anger in the family proved more difficult. We were all too aware of the rat-hole nature of addiction. Although the "cure," had slipped away from Steve yet again, I decided we had to do it. It was a matter of life or death. Neither my husband nor my ex-husband was enthusiastic about another go-round, but I finally decided to go ahead anyway even if I couldn't get their support. I just made an executive decision. It was a "Mother thing." To me, there was a direct line from "Steve is my son," to "This is my money, and I can spend it on him if I want to."

The next step was getting Steve to agree to go. For several months, he had been denying his relapse. He was convinced that external events caused his problems: a disagreeable boss, a mean landlord, etc., etc.–

the old victim line of thinking. Nothing is the addict's responsibility. Everything that happens to him is somebody else's fault.

I didn't have a clue about how to convince Steve to go. The director of the facility suggested an intervention: "We can recommend someone for you. If you want to talk to him, I can give you his phone number."

I had heard of interventions: family members and close friends gather around the addict to tell him why they won't have any more to do with him unless he gets sober. An intervention means trying to leave only one way out for the addict, to go to treatment, but the real horsepower comes from the show of love and determination from the group.

When Will, the interventionist, heard Steve's story, he told me it was very much like his own. He told me things about the way Steve behaved that I knew could only come from personal experience, from the inside out. What he said seemed truer than many things doctors and psychologists had told me. What he said was exactly what had happened to us.

"It's also important not to tell Steve in advance that you're doing an intervention," he advised. "He won't show up for it if he's denying he has a problem. Tell him I'm a counselor and we are merely having a general session about his depression."

That sounded workable. Years earlier, Steve had been diagnosed with manic depression and had struggled with that throughout his life. My father had had deep bouts of depression and, at the age of 54, took his own life. Steve had attempted suicide when he was thirteen years old.

That event led to his first hospitalization, and that memory hung over me like the sword of Damocles.

"Here's what I want you to do," advised Will. "Talk to other people in the family and set a date. If all of you can come down here, we can have the meeting in Los Angeles where Steve is."

He gave me other instructions about how to prepare for the intervention. Everyone in the family would write a letter to Steve telling him positive things about how we felt toward him. The letters were for support, not blame.

"Give my name and number to everyone in the family. Tell them to call me if they have questions, or if they just want to talk. I want them to be comfortable with this process."

Steve had moved out of his girlfriend's house, and I had paid for a week's lodging for him at a cheap motel in Canoga Park. He was trying to convince me I should give him some money for a fresh start, so I used that as the reason for the family 'meeting.' I told him I had found a counselor who might be able to help him with his recurring depression. Steve was suspicious.

"Is this an intervention?"

"No, just an evaluation session."

It was the only time I had ever lied to any of my kids. The words almost stuck in my throat, but I got them out because I felt his life depended on it.

We set a date about a week away. I drove down with my husband Craig; my ex-husband Russ, and our eldest son Dan.

The next morning, we had a pre-intervention meeting with Will so he could meet everybody, hear our letters and go over the ground rules. We were all jumpy and on edge. Everyone had a lot to say. Resentments and bad feelings that had built up over the years crowded at each other for expression. One memory inspired the recollection of another. The "briefing" session devolved into a "dumping" session.

My anxiety level soared. "This was a big mistake," I thought. "Nothing good can possibly come of this."

Trying to remain positive, the interventionist reminded us: "Remember you are here to show support for Steve and get him into treatment. I know you're all angry and you've been ripped off for years and years, but this is not the time to vent about that. If you start arguing with him, he'll spook and won't go in. We're here to solve problems."

The family needed the pep talk because whenever we talked about Steve, we tended to revert to war stories. The war stories were our experiences over the years; they explained and justified our anger. They had gotten us where we were that day.

"Now, what I'd like to happen is to have the meeting with Steve this afternoon, get him to agree to go, and then I'll get on a plane with him tonight and escort him up north."

Wait a minute, I thought. What happens to Steve's car, the stuff he has in his motel room? What does he have to pack, etc. There were more loose ends. And I balked at the previously-unmentioned need for plane tickets. I was beginning to feel money hemorrhaging: cost of treatment, cost of interventionist, and now we seemed to be looking at hundreds more dollars for travel expenses. I guess I hadn't thought through how Steve was going to get to treatment. I had assumed that we would pack his stuff into our van and take him up ourselves.

We decided to let the question of transportation go for the moment because we had more immediate challenges, like getting through the next few hours.

We left Mike's house and caravanned out to Steve's motel to pick him up. It looked like every other cheap motel in the Los Angeles area. An assortment of mostly worn-out older cars was parked in front of the two dozen or so units. I secretly feared that Steve would not keep his appointment with us, so I was relieved when we spotted Steve's MG. The manager directed me to a room on the first floor. I knocked, waited, and knocked again. Steve spoke through the closed door:

"Just wait out there. I'll be right out." I waited. After a few minutes, I called through the door.

"Steve, may I please come in and use your bathroom? We have a bit of a drive to get to the place where we're going to have the meeting, and I need to go!"

Reluctantly, he unlocked the door and pointed to the bathroom. No wonder he didn't want to have me come in—the room was a mess! Clothes were everywhere on the floor and all over the furniture. I don't think Steve had made the bed the entire week. The bathroom was the same. Toiletries scattered among more clothes, all over the counter, all over the floor. When I came out of the bathroom, he hurried me back out the door.

"Wait for me outside. I'll just be a moment."

Will had driven ahead to the place where he had arranged to have the intervention. It was near the beach, about half an hour away. We had all hoped Steve would get in our car so we could take him, but he insisted on driving his MG. I wasn't at all comfortable with that. In his condition, would he be able to drive in traffic? Was he able to follow us? I thought there was a good chance he was incapable of following the directions, but he didn't leave another option. He refused to get into the van with the rest of us, and his car didn't have a passenger seat. Nobody could even ride with him to make sure he got there. This development began looking like a big hole in the plan. I felt that Steve could split any moment. Well, at least only the family was present at the motel. I think if Will had shown up with us, Steve would have smelled an intervention and bolted.

It seemed like a very long drive to me. I kept my head turned backwards to make sure that Steve's car was still following us. Twenty miles later, his MG was right behind ours as we turned into a large conference center. We found Will's car at the designated building and made our way inside. So far, so good. Things appeared to be what we had told Steve we were doing, just a family counseling session. Will was waiting for us in a pleasantly furnished meeting room with glass doors that opened to an inner courtyard.

By the time we were all seated around the room, my heart was pounding so hard I could barely hear what Will was saying, but after some introductory remarks he called on us to read our letters. It was very emotional and would have been very powerful if Steve had been receptive. Instead, when the last letter was read, Steve turned to Will and asked the question he had asked me on the phone a week earlier.

"Is this an intervention?"

Will didn't lie, but he didn't answer the question directly. His evasion was obvious and I think that's when he lost the upper hand. Steve got him on the defensive and took advantage of it to launch a litany of excuses for his situation.

Others in the family did not react kindly. Their anger was too close to the surface to keep submerged. The intervention turned into a blaming session, not the loving base of support it was supposed to be.

Will asked Steve to step outside and smoke a cigarette with him. He signaled to the rest of us to stay behind. I was so angry and confused I couldn't talk to anybody. I got up and walked into the other room to try to collect my thoughts. This was not going well. It was practically out of control. The problem was that, even in his sick state, Steve was smarter than this interventionist and, at that very moment, was outmaneuvering him.

They talked for a very long time. Occasionally one of them chuckled. That seemed to be a good sign. At least it wasn't argumentative. The rest of us cooled our heels while we waited inside. There wasn't much we could do but pace or sit. We couldn't talk about the reason we were there, and talking about anything else seemed pointless and silly.

Will came back in and explained that Steve agreed he needed to go to treatment, but needed a couple of days to straighten out his affairs. Steve did not return to the meeting room, but stayed outside. When we walked out to him, he didn't say anything about going or not going to treatment. He didn't ask what facility we had in mind. He showed no interest in the subject at all.

"Would you like to come back with us and have dinner, Steve?" I asked, trying to hold on to him for just a little bit longer. I hated the idea of his going back to that awful motel room. I hated the idea of his going back to the bong factory even more. I wanted to protect him and thought he would be safe if he would stay with us even if it were just for the evening.

"No, I have to meet somebody. I'll see you later. Don't worry about me."

"Steve, please go to treatment and take care of yourself. Can't you see we all want you to get well."

"Yeah, I know. I'll probably go in. I know I need to go. I just can't go right now. I have some things to do."

It sounded like more delaying tactics and denial, however, Will assured us that he thought Steve would go in soon and promised to call every day until it happened.

I was not at all assured. I asked Steve to at least have dinner with us; Mike knew a place on the way back to town. Steve said he'd think about it, but it didn't surprise me when we turned off the highway to pull into the parking lot of the restaurant and Steve's car kept right on going. As I saw him disappear into traffic, my stomach clutched with fear. For all I knew I would never see him again.

We were a pretty gloomy bunch at dinner, which I'm sure was very tasty, but I couldn't enjoy anything. The next day we returned to the Bay Area.

Will called us every day that week to report on his attempts to talk with Steve. Every day Steve either had an excuse about why he couldn't go that particular day or sometimes didn't even bother to answer the phone. Will even made a couple of trips to the motel and knocked on Steve's door with no results. Then Will left for another intervention, another family in the same crisis we were in.

Contrary to his former advice, Will asked me to pay for Steve's motel room one more day after one more day until a week had passed after the intervention.

Steve was still out and Will kept saying he thought Steve was very close to going in.

We learned later that Steve was trying to work out other living arrangements but couldn't and decided to give up and go to treatment.

Will had offered to follow him in his own car to make sure he got there, but now Will was helping another client. Mike offered to store Steve's MG and drive him up. Steve refused that, too. Dan offered to drive down to Los Angeles again and pick him up, but Steve insisted that he could get there on his own. He called me to say that he would be leaving the next day.

I asked Mike to see that Steve's gas tank was filled and that he had some money for food on the trip, but we were wary of putting cash directly into his pockets because we feared he wouldn't use it for travel expenses.

Craig and I drove to the treatment center the day Steve said he would check in. We wanted to be there when he arrived so we could pay for his treatment and collect his animals he said he was bringing with him. We waited until ten o'clock that evening, but Steve did not show up and did not call. It was a four-hour drive to the center from Los Angeles, and the conclusion we drew was that he had shined us on again.

When we got home that night, however, there was a message from Mike saying that Steve had called him from some gas station on I-5 where he was stranded. One of Steve's tires had blown out and his MG had to be towed. Mike used his own credit card to take care of that crisis and we began a vigil hoping for word that Steve would make it to treatment without other problems.

I hope Steve will write his own story about that journey. It's a story that may best be described as "disaster narrowly averted." Every element in the story was a formula for failure. Steve's MG was in ratty shape, probably not even legal on the highway. The two kittens were loose in the car. Steve says one of them spent the entire trip wrapped around the back of his neck in total panic. The other one careened around inside the car and at one point escaped and ran off into an onion field. Steve was able to catch her and she did make it but vocalized her extreme unhappiness. The monitor lizard was the only one who didn't seem to be upset; Cyn made the trip zipped up in a gym bag and snoozed the entire time.

As for Steve himself, months later he told me that the day before he left, he had gotten a "final payment" from his employer and smoked it all the way to treatment. It was his own farewell party to drugs and alcohol because he knew what would follow. Apparently, it's fairly typical behavior for addicts. Blow out before you dry out. I do not even pretend to understand. I am thankful, however, that there was a strong voice inside of Steve that eventually got him into treatment again.

I thank all the gods that be for Steve having finally been able to defeat his demons, although I know it's risky saying *finally*. Steve and others like him will have to wrestle with their demons every day as long as they live. The important thing for Steve is that all those years of drug abuse apparently did not damage his brain or his soul; he is still as smart and loving as he ever was. He was always able to manipulate people to get his way. When he was using, all he wanted was to get more drugs, so his abilities and skills were used for selfish and destructive purposes.

Now–clean, sober and happy–Steve is using his considerable skills to give people their lives back. He is helping other families with interventions so they can get their addicts into treatment.

During his time in treatment, he learned how to *solve* life's daily problems instead of anesthetizing himself against them.

He has always been highly intuitive, able to *read* other people and now he uses that skill to assist families and friends of addicts in doing what they need to do.

This book will tell you more about his work. I have been fascinated by his stories, and I'm glad he has written them down. I think he has a lot to say, a lot of wisdom to impart. I know that he doesn't always follow the formula used in his own intervention: the letters, the family circle meeting. He doesn't wait for family members to call him; he calls them and gets them to talk in depth about the addict and then he develops a plan of action, designed for that particular family. He is creative and original. He says he has to be because there's no easy formula; every case concerns a unique individual and a family with its own strengths and weaknesses. I admire his work and am proud to be part of this book. Maybe our story will help someone else. I hope so.

To those who love an addict–whether it's your child, spouse, sibling, or friend–my message is: always keep hope alive. If one treatment doesn't work, look for another. Give yourself permission to spend the family legacy on treatment; we don't get many chances to buy a life back. If we can do it we should do it because to hesitate might mean to lose that chance, forever.

Into The Lion's Den

"The greatest obstacle to discovery is not ignorance,
it is the illusion of knowledge. "
~ *Daniel Boorstein*

Prior to graduating from rehab, I spent some time working with the program director. He had populated the facility largely by doing interventions. Many of my peers were his "products."

Knowing I was interested, he encouraged me. He took me to lunch several times and did his best to enlighten me on how he felt an intervention should be done. I even witnessed an important aspect of his work up close, purely by chance.

A family crowded into his office while I was in the waiting area. Shortly, I heard loud voices from behind his closed door. It was the mother and the director, but I had missed the lead story: The family's son, who had been brought there to start the program, had run out of the office and down the hill in a rebellious fit. The facility was near Salinas, California in an agricultural town, so even if he ran all the way to the edge of the property, expanses of farms would still surround him.

I could hear John, the director, responding to something the mom said, "Making everything into a crisis is how your son _controls_ you. It's how he has *been* controlling you."

She replied, half hearing what he said and half waiting for him to mount a full-scale manhunt, "Well, what are you planning to *do* about it!?" Her voice wavered between indignation and a need for answers.

John was not what she was used to, and his simple, spot-on observation about her son using crises as means of control set her afloat; it was true and she knew it. Everyone else in the room—her husband and her other two boys—knew it. They were used to a very different pattern, a lot like my own family, the mom as the centerpiece and the drug addicted son, a walking catalyst. He would react with a crisis, causing *her* to panic. She would then transfer that state of panic to those around her.

That's what I used to do, I thought. First, create a panic; second, make something or someone wrong…in this case, the kid was targeting treatment; third, make sure Mom is freaked out enough to be in serious doubt about whatever "it" is; fourth, whip out an alternative plan; fifth, insist that if they don't go along with it, some other crisis will befall everyone.

John did not disappoint. He spoke with confidence, almost boredom, as if he was saying it for the hundredth time that day. "The fact is, your son has nowhere to go. Let's get some dinner and finish the tour. If we don't hear from him within a couple of hours we'll send someone to look for him, but for now, we just wait for him to come back." Then he added, "He needs to know things are different this time." John's next words have stayed with me, *"You need to be the family he's not used to seeing."*

Just as John predicted, within the hour the kid came back, taking no notice of me as he skulked through the front doors and into the director's office. He immediately began railing against his mother. He went from rage to apathy, to promises of change to promises he'd never speak to them again. But now the family was acutely, if not painfully, aware of this very mechanism; he didn't have a chance.

Shortly the paperwork was signed, and the family drove down the hill without him. The kid did fine in the program–great, as I recall.

The time was coming for me to graduate. The treatment center staff offered me a job but I declined. I wanted to go out on my own. I can't remember who mentioned it first, but I remember my family encouraged me to try my hand at doing interventions. I thought, *why not?* My years as a drug addict, combined with my years managing high-paced environments meant I could probably handle just about any situation. I didn't think I'd be surprised by much. I can now say, after over 15 years as an interventionist, I greatly underestimated the spectrum of theater my career would provide.

I bugged the admissions counselor to see if she could get me an intervention. I was excited and terrified of it actually happening. Doing something that many people thought was impossible appealed to my sense of adventure, a challenge to my abilities, but the thought that I might fail a family who was trying to save the life of someone they love was frightening.

Two days later, Stacey, the admissions counselor, handed me a piece of paper with a name and phone number scrawled on it and said, "Here you go, Steve. They are expecting your call. Let me know how it goes, and don't worry about it if you don't get the guy in. It sounds like a long shot."

I took the number and called. A woman answered. She described her son, Sam, 34, who had not been in communication with her or with the rest of the family for about two months. They knew where he was and had some idea of what he was doing, which she described to me between emotional silences.

Over the course of several years, a crystal meth addiction had left Sam hostile and isolated. Currently, he was locked in his house and rumored to be wanted by the FBI for manufacturing and trafficking. At first I thought she might be overly dramatic but, after I spoke with other family members including Sam's father who had connections in law enforcement, I suspected the worst.

I drove to Oakland to meet with the family. I had their check in my shirt pocket, ready to return it if I found myself in over my head.

I spent the trip trying to remember everything the program director had told me. I had also scanned a couple of books on the subject. A lot of the information I got from the director and the books steered me toward approaching the intervention as a meeting with the addict, during which he is confronted with evidence of what he's been doing. During this quasi-ambush, he is told that he is loved but that his negative behavior is affecting the family to the point where the family now needed to disconnect if he, the addict, is not willing to go to treatment. In addition to this, the family is also tasked with getting the addict to admit he needs help.

To be honest, it never made a lot of sense to me that that would be the way a professional would approach *every single intervention,* but I was willing to give it a try and, as a novice, who was I to argue? Besides, this one-size-fits-all approach had worked for many families. Why not this one?

I arrived at Sam's family's home as the afternoon sun was coloring everything in a warm, amber light. Even the stark white house I arrived at looked like it had been frosted in butter-cream. A beautiful maple dressed in new spring foliage seemed to wink at me as I approached the front door.

I knocked. A woman in her early twenties answered, one of Sam's sisters. I sobered up quickly to the scene inside. Sam's mother and other sister were seated on the couch, and appeared to be comforting each other. One of Sam's brothers was pacing around the room nervously. He was talking, apparently to everyone but no one seemed to be listening. Sam's father was a lone figure standing in the corner of the room. His arms were crossed. He looked as if he didn't want to be there. Sam's mother looked up at me, a handkerchief in her hand.

I admit, I was *damned* nervous. Here was the first family I had ever even met with, in a state of extreme distress and it was up to me to offer them *more* than hope. *Could I?* I raced over details in my mind as we made introductions.

Sam had locked himself in his house, which he owned. The family had not heard from him in over two months. According to various sources in contact with him, he was doing methamphetamine. They were told Sam had been "remodeling" his house.

Ha! I thought. *I can relate to that.* I immediately understood what they were describing from first-hand experience.

I knew what Sam was doing and that, by now, he would be a conflicted mess of drug-fueled, manic highs and withdrawal-fueled, suicidal lows. I realized that, despite the fact I'd never met the guy, I knew *a lot* about Sam. I knew the condition he was in at any rate. In that moment, I felt I might be able to help him. I had to try.

As warm, deep orange sunlight poured through the windows, I started to feel calm; I *knew* what this family was describing to me. Their nervous and disconnected state was so familiar I found it almost comforting. The things they were describing in Sam were qualities my family would have described in me. They were the exact details of my behavior for many years. I mentally locked their check up in my pocket, now believing I *might* succeed.

I thought about the family, about everybody in the room looking to me for answers. I thought about Sam in a state of mania, scenarios of suicide, lost love, pain, hope, despair, all sweeping through his mind like the tides, his emotions doing swan dives from the surrounding cliffs. Been there.

The feeling of calm I had was replaced by a different kind of nervousness. It felt like stage fright.

I needed to *think*. I excused myself and walked outside.

I was missing information. I needed to know more about Sam, his situation, and his past. I needed to find a hook to catch him on. I needed to know more about his circumstances other than the fact that he was an addict. That was too generic. Besides, I wasn't hired so I could lecture Sam about meth or impress him with my knowledge of it. I wasn't there to get him to admit to anything either. It just didn't strike me as relevant. In fact, it would be outright problematic with very few upsides *if any*, especially in the condition Sam was in. The only thing that mattered to me at that point was getting Sam to the front doors of the program. I needed to put something together that was going to *work,* and I made a decision that would shape my career for years to come.

I decided to put aside everything I had read and everything I had been told about interventions. I cleared my mind and focused on one point in the universe, which was Sam agreeing to treatment and getting into my car. Then I worked backward through the events that would most likely lead him there.

I am not suggesting that a family ambush is a bad idea. It can work well but in *this* case I needed to be creative, not formulaic. It seemed unlikely that we would be able to pull off initiating a family meeting, much less get through it. This was a pivotal moment for me. The decision I made was to discard the idea of this being a classic intervention. I was being nudged into adopting a broader viewpoint, and a simplified one. I just needed to get Sam <u>into</u> treatment. However it needed to be done, that became my only goal. That's what I was there to do: meetings or not, his admitting to anything or not, letters read by family members *or not*.

I walked back in and asked where Sam lived, if he lived alone, did he have a girlfriend, did he have a job, what did he care about, was he a musician, did he have pets, did he have a storage unit, did he have any money—if so, where and how much—who were his friends, what was the most recent story about him they had heard, did he have a car, did he rent or own his house. The answers would become the foundation for developing a strategy designed just for Sam.

As the answers came in, I noticed something: Several of the answers were different depending on who was doing the answering. I made another key decision that would serve me well over the following years which was to talk to family members individually and let them speak their minds, not only about the addict but about each other. I had no question what Sam's condition was, but I needed to know the condition of his family as well. You don't want someone, at the halfway point, to suddenly agree that the addict *doesn't* need treatment. That can be a *big* problem, especially if it could have been predicted it in the first place. If you have someone who might throw a wrench into the mix, either get him on board or exclude him.

When I asked whether Sam had been in a romantic relationship recently, both of Sam's parents averted their eyes and shook their heads while both of his sisters looked at me and nodded. Sam's father explained that Sabrina, Sam's ex, had been hurt too much by Sam and would never be willing to participate in anything having to do with him and that they, as Sam's parents, weren't comfortable asking her to get involved. The look in the eyes of his sisters told me something different. I needed to know what. I asked his sister Lisa if the two of us could go for a walk. As soon as we were outside, I asked her about Sabrina. She said Sam was totally heartbroken over her, and Sam was a complete wreck after their breakup. That's when he isolated himself and the drugs took hold. I didn't have to hear much else. I asked Lisa for Sabrina's phone number and called.

Even as an addict, I have always been a romantic. I have even been known to write a love poem or two. The description of Sam struck me as very similar, not only in the sense that he was using meth, but he sounded like a romantic as well.

Sabrina, however, began our conversation by making it abundantly clear she didn't want to have anything to do with Sam. She told me she didn't even like him as a person anymore. She certainly did not want to be around him. He had betrayed her. She didn't trust him. He was a mess. He smelled bad. He was a drug addict. I remained silent while she listed off the guy's faults. Again, echoes of my own family using these adjectives to describe me before I went into treatment flowed through my head as Sabrina continued her unapologetic description.

I responded by telling her I didn't need her to have anything to do with Sam after this. I just wanted her to participate in the intervention so we could get him into treatment, hopefully saving his life. Sabrina, satisfied it wouldn't lead to any kind of ongoing involvement, agreed to meet with Sam. The two of us would go to Sam's house and try to speak with him on our own, without any family. My going out on a limb and calling Sabrina, contrary to what the parents felt comfortable with, had now provided me with a potent angle.

I told the family about my talk with Sabrina and what she had agreed to do. After a few stunned moments, they seemed almost disappointed, like they had geared up for a very difficult few days and here I come and take the wind out of their sails. No one argued with my decision however, so, off Sabrina and I went.

We arrived at Sam's house and I knocked on the door. After a brief silence, Sam grunted something from inside. Sabrina spoke through the door saying she'd be happy to give him a chance to gather himself together if he'd come out and visit for a little while. A few minutes later, Sam made his appearance.

As he opened the door, stale air blew across my face from inside the house. Sam himself was emaciated. His clothes were encrusted with dirt and paint splatters, but his focus was on Sabrina, as I'd hoped. She did exactly what I had asked. She told Sam she just wanted him to listen to what I had to say, and that he didn't have to say anything. Sam happily obliged. He put on his game face but–it was sad to watch–he was in a wretched state.

I started out a little apologetically, excusing my presence there. That brought Sam's guard down slightly. I set the table with the problems I knew Sam was facing. I began by describing my own struggle with meth, with my family, with the law, with depression, and the resulting loss of opportunities, relationships and self-worth.

You don't want to oversell the program to the point where the addict takes a huge loss on it when he gets there, but you do want him to feel it's somewhere he might like to be. With that in mind, I described the program in a way I thought would be enticing.

I did not emphasize the therapy. Therapy doesn't necessarily sell tickets as well as *aesthetics*. Swimming pools sell tickets. Satellite TV sells tickets. Good food sells tickets. Getting away from the parents (kids, spouse, etc.). An island in the sun sells tickets. Horseback riding, golf, yoga, a weight room. You can turn a morning walk into a person getting his or her health back if you want to. You shouldn't outright lie about the amenities at a program, but if it sounds like prison camp the addict will not want to go. You may be thinking to yourself that the program you've chosen doesn't have any redeeming qualities you can really sell. In that case, you may need to look for a different program, but you probably just need to try harder and look more closely at the program you've chosen. Every program in the world has some aspect that is there to provide relief, recreation, encourage social interaction, fitness, and so on.

Many family members are so angry by the time the intervention starts that they overlook this and, instead, approach things from the angle that the addict should be grateful and deserves whatever hardships may await...Good luck with that.

I told Sam I was there because the people who loved him believed that he was so much more than the life he was currently living. His family missed him and wanted the old Sam back. I told him that's all anyone wanted, including Sabrina. Sam stood tense for a few moments; then he slowly started sobbing. Sabrina walked over and looked Sam in the eyes and said, "I'm asking you to give it a <u>try</u>, Sam. If you don't want to stay, then don't stay, but if you don't at least try then we'll never know what might happen, will we?" She put her hand lightly on his shoulder. His cheeks flushed. Sam started nodding his head before she'd finished the sentence, "Yes, yes, I'll try."

The important thing to me wasn't whether Sabrina bent the truth by giving Sam hope for something she and I knew would never happen; the important thing was that we got Sam to the program. She could apologize later for how she did it. It was time this guy got out of the hell he'd gotten himself into.

I told Sam a couple more things that would shape my future success. First I told him, "We don't even have to talk to your parents about this. Get your things together, pack them up and we'll go. I'll make the arrangements." By doing this, I let him off the hook in terms of having to go through his family in order to go to the program. I'm not sure he'd thought that far ahead but he again nodded his approval.

My car was parked out front. I motioned to it. "Look, do what you want," I said. "I used to smoke meth in a bong factory...where we made the meth! So I get it. I'm just your ride, Man." I tried to make it as easy for him as possible.

It actually took Sam about 10 hours to get ready. He kept going back and forth. In fact, it took him nine hours just to pack two bags. As an ex-meth addict, that didn't surprise me. I just waited patiently. I knew he was "tweaking," so I called him on it, a little bit jokingly. Eventually we got into the car and left.

I took the scenic route just as I'd promised, right out to the coast and down Highway 1, Sam smiling the entire way, the top down, wind in his hair, his leg up on the door.

On the way, I realized something. He was happy. He was happy to be free from the house. He was happy to have been given time to pack. He was also happy to be able to smoke his meth if he wanted to. I think he took a couple of hits in a gas station bathroom. When the subject came up, I told him I didn't care what he did as long as I didn't have to watch him do it. This guy was just happy to be going to a place without having to go through the gauntlet of his estranged family to get there.

Another thing I learned that day and have seen confirmed time and time again since is that if you try to police an addict too tightly before his first day of treatment, flush his drugs down the toilet to make him stop using, all you're going to do is antagonize him and maybe flush the intervention down the toilet as well. You're not solving the big picture.

Make it as easy for the person as possible.

I put my heart and soul into every intervention I do, and most of the time I succeed because of that one thing; I approach each addict, each situation as if I'm saving myself.

Part II

Intervention 101

Sources of Information

"In your thirst for knowledge, don't drown in the information."

~ Anthony J. D'Angelo

In your run-up to doing an intervention, you are bound to get advice about *how* an intervention should be done, but be forewarned: A family member, friend or someone you met at a support group who's been involved in one or two interventions isn't *necessarily* giving you advice you want to bet the farm on—maybe yes, maybe no.

I'm not suggesting you should reject what you hear simply because it's coming from someone without a lot of experience. Every piece of data or suggestion *can* be valuable, but it's important to keep things in perspective. Get the back story.

For example, you might be advised to never use an addict's "ex" during an intervention because the person advising you had an intervention go south because of it. On the other hand, many ex-spouses, ex-girlfriends and ex-boyfriends have been involved in interventions with great success. No two situations are alike. What was a bad idea for one might be a great idea for someone else. It all boils down to what will most likely work for the person you are trying to help.

Mainstream Intervention Models

I've read books about interventions and can't say I agree with everything in them. In fact, there are quite a number of "mainstream" ideas floating around which I consider to be counterproductive.

For example, by far the most well-known book on interventions advises that anyone who has an active addiction or alcohol dependency *not* be involved in an intervention for someone else. If I'd followed that advice I would not have succeeded in a good number of interventions. One Georgia family is a good example: A woman from Atlanta hired me to get her heroin-addicted son into rehab. She and the addict's sister were to be my support team. The addict himself lived with his father, a blackout drunk.

I found out the addict was stealing money from his father. The father, who was on his own emotional and chemical rollercoaster, knew about it. I took advantage of that and told him all about the program his ex-wife had agreed to pay for. I focused on the amenities and aesthetics. I told him how nice it was which of course infuriated him because he was already angry about the money his son was stealing from him. He happily came to the courthouse with me where I began helping him file for a restraining order against his son, who would end up with nowhere left to go except treatment. When we found out that the county we were in required the sheriff to serve the restraining order within two hours, the father paused, turned to me and said, "We don't need this. *I* will get him to go."

He was so angry his face had turned bright red and looked like it was about to burst. It was all I could do to keep up with him as I followed him in my rental car. We parked out in front of his house. He went inside while I waited in my car. A few minutes later the kid came flying out of the side door, waving his shirt and yelling back at the house. He made his way over to my car, got in and slumped down into the passenger seat with his arms crossed. He growled at me, "I guess I have to go with you or my father's going to have me arrested." Long story short, we were on a plane to the treatment center *that night*.

If I had followed the advice in the book, I would never have worked with the father and would probably not have gotten his son into rehab.

One of the shortest interventions I ever did was for a young man in Alabama. He was 18 and living at home. His mother told me she would buy him a brand-new Mustang if he went to treatment *and* graduated.

I think our conversation lasted all of five minutes—the kid couldn't wait to go!

Of course there aren't a lot of families in that position, but that isn't the point. The point is that we did what *worked* using the resources available. And, in case you're wondering, no I do *not* think it's a good idea to give a drug addict a brand-new car for going to treatment for a couple of months. Maybe a used car, and *keep it in your name!*

At the end of the day, your only purpose during an intervention is to play your pieces so the addict goes into treatment. Whether you do it in two moves or two hundred is irrelevant. The only thing that matters is that your addict arrives at the program and that the program is the best choice for him in terms of its effectiveness.

Do what you think will work, not what people tell you you're *supposed* to do, or should *never* do. An intervention is not a game of absolutes. Give yourself permission to use everything you learn or to throw it all out and start over. Encourage people to share ideas, but stay away from the *supposed-to* or *everyone-knows* statements. If I had stuck to what *everyone-knows*, I would not be nearly as successful in my work.

If someone in your clan is quietly thinking to himself, "I could get him into treatment if we didn't have to do this whole family meeting thing..." or someone suggests, "Hey, he'd go if we_____." *Get a hold of those ideas.*

Rehearse them and see how they play out; make the necessary adjustments. Improvise. Don't gravitate toward the easier formula just because it's easier. Find the *winning* formula, even if it is more difficult.

The Issue of Proof

"I'm in favor of drug testing, as long as it's multiple choice"

~ Kurt Rambis

It's common for families to get stuck proving that their beloved addict is really an addict. They feel a need to convince themselves or others that action needs to be taken, so they do things like search the addict's room, follow him around with GPS, smell his breath, or round up empty bottles, baggies, hypodermic needles, prescriptions, and other evidence of drug use. They believe that, if confronted with it, the addict will be unable to deny his problem, realize he must do something about it, and then do it.

Well, I have news for you: Addicts can invalidate, obfuscate and cast doubt on seemingly indisputable evidence with such alacrity that they can stand there with crack pipe in hand and categorically deny they use drugs.

Here's the good news: You are reading this because you are concerned about someone and want to help him. So you do *not* need to prove it. Move on to finding a program and getting him, or her, into it.

An intervention is *not* a process of discovery. It is not a time to "get answers." Proof of drug use is only valuable to the extent it motivates *you* to move things forward, so if at this point you are not sure that there is a problem that merits treatment, then you are not ready to do an intervention.

If you are certain there is a problem, put the urine test away. Put the pipes away. The aluminum foil goes in the recycling bin.

The only things that belong in the intervention are the letters, the offer, a reminder of who the addict is as a person, a full-color description of the aesthetics of the program and some serious organization time.

I don't even talk about the person's drug use if I don't have to. If an offer of rehabilitation is on the table, it's obvious what everyone is talking about.

The world of the addict is full of shadows and fear. He knows he's not tracking with reality; he knows he's in danger of arrest, of incarceration, or being discovered. He knows that his drug use stigmatizes him in the eyes of society and of his family. But putting these things on display during an intervention is probably a bad idea with little potential upside. An intervention should not be allowed to turn into a kangaroo court.

The addict is already feeling as wrong as he can possibly be. He does not need to be *proved* wrong; *he needs to be given a way out*. This may go against Uncle Mike who needs to say his piece, or other family members seeking to justify their treatment of the addict or to condemn his treatment of them, but such actions will only create a greater rift in the family and literally serve no purpose.

If your loved one has lost his way, focus your efforts on finding a solution and present it as enticingly as possible. In fact, if the issue of proving the addiction comes up, *push that conversation aside*. Instead, make the point that you are not there to judge or evaluate whether the person is an addict, but you are there to let him know that you are no longer willing to participate in his self-destructive behavior.

Legal/Medical

"Don't do drugs because if you do you'll go to prison,
and drugs are really expensive in prison."

~ John Hardwick

This section is in no way intended as legal advice. If you want legal advice, you should consult an attorney, but I have some experience in this area that you might find helpful.

Legal cases, warrants or pending court dates tend to have much better outcomes when they are dealt with while the addict or alcoholic is *in treatment* rather than trying to resolve things in advance. I have found this to be so universally true that when I learn an addict has arrest warrants, pending court cases and so on, I immediately start working to get that person into the treatment facility *before* he is due again in court.

When an addict goes into a treatment facility and that treatment facility, in turn, contacts the court, judges tend to be very understanding and flexible. This is especially true if the case is drug or alcohol related.

If there is a probation officer involved, *I do not recommend asking his permission to go to rehab beforehand.* It's counterproductive to begin with the probation officer as opposed to getting your addict into treatment beforehand and the treatment center then contacting the court clerk directly. The reason for this is that probation officers are junior to the judge in the case (everyone is), and probation officers who like to wield what power they've been given don't always have the most productive outcomes in mind. Even if the addict has a probation officer who might be willing to help, going about it that way involves a lot more red tape and there's literally no upside. The treatment center will be able to contact the judge directly through the court clerk. So, probation officer or not, court dates or not, bench warrants or not, the first course of action is to get the person *into* the program.

Typically when a judge finds out the person is in a program, he will order a *continuance;* this gives the person a break from having to deal with the court date or warrant. The person is usually given time until he graduates from the program, at which point the judge may be more favorably disposed to deal with the case leniently.

It works the other way around as well. If the person leaves the treatment center prematurely, the court is notified. Fear of being arrested can be a great incentive for addicts to stay in the program. I'm not suggesting that the simple act of going into a treatment center means unconditional forgiveness by the legal system. Obviously, if your addict is on the run as a fugitive or is on parole or something of that nature, that falls well out of the scope of this chapter, and ultimately it's all up to the judge. In many cases, however, charges are even dismissed upon the person's successful completion of a treatment program, or shortly thereafter. It happened to me.

When I went to treatment, I had four charges: a federal trafficking charge, two felony possession-with-intent-to-sell charges and one misdemeanor possession charge. Because they were all drug related, my lawyer requested diversion (also known as Drug Court, Prop 36 or alternative sentencing, in many cases a one-time get-out-of-jail-free card for drug offenders willing to attend an approved treatment program and who have never had diversion in the past), although my attorney told me he had never seen a judge allow diversion for two felonies *and* a federal charge. Diversion is typically reserved for middle-of-the-road drug cases. In any event, I wasn't about to argue.

Upon successfully graduating from treatment, I was placed on the equivalent of probation. I also began doing interventions. The judge was aware of this because I was constantly requesting special permission to leave the state in order to do them. Six months after I graduated from treatment, I was standing in her courtroom once again. As I stood there in the middle of the courtroom full of people, the judge looked up at me and said, "Mr. Bruno, my understanding is that you have been helping families for the past six months and you were in treatment for close to six months prior to that, is that correct?"

I nodded my head, "Yes, Your Honor."

She looked down momentarily at the piece of paper she held in her hand and then continued, speaking a little louder and addressing the entire room, "Why don't we all get up and give Mr. Bruno a hand." Then back to me, "I'm going to go ahead and dismiss *all* of your cases." She motioned for everyone in the courtroom to applaud.

The call for applause was unusual, but most judges, whether they are in upstate New York or downtown Los Angeles, become much friendlier toward a person's case if he or she is in or has completed a treatment program.

Many courts view time in treatment as time served, and most quality treatment centers will either have an attorney or someone who deals with legal matters, so if you have a pending court date or warrant, get the person *into* the program before doing anything else. The exception to this would be if the addict is on parole (which is *not* the same as probation) *and* the treatment program is in a different state.

In terms of pending court dates, every facility I have ever worked with routinely reschedules court appearances for clients. Therefore, it's far better to get an addict or alcoholic into the program where he can sober up and work with staff members to address his legal issues. This is *much* more effective than waiting and expecting a using addict or alcoholic to handle things (in most cases, *while* continuing to break the law).

Restraining Orders: When, How and Whom

I use Temporary Restraining Orders, or TROs, but only in extreme circumstances.

A TRO is an order from a judge to prevent a person from being near another person, place, or thing or from acting in a certain manner. It is very useful for getting a person out of a house or apartment when a long eviction process is not realistic. For example, a person can apply for a restraining order and, if granted, the person named is *immediately* ordered by a judge to stay at least 100 feet away from another individual, a residence and/or a vehicle.

TROs are granted to people who show that their safety or life is in danger from another person, are typically granted immediately and are immediately enforceable.

Before you ask for a TRO, educate yourself about the details of the local restrictions and requirements surrounding them. A restraining order must be requested in person at the county courthouse but the requirements vary. You can look them up online, but make certain you are looking at the regulations applicable in *your* county, or call your local superior court clerk.

As I said, TROs are for the extreme situation–they're not a first course of action–but if the person you're trying to help is threatening you, *or if you feel you can make the case,* don't hesitate to go down to the courthouse and apply for a TRO. If you're not sure whether you qualify, keep this one thing in mind: *A judge will <u>not</u> grant a TRO because of drug use or even drug dealing. A TRO is only granted if you can make the case there is a threat to your safety.* Whatever details your story may include, it must lead the judge to that conclusion in order for you to be granted a restraining order.

A TRO is usually enforceable for about two weeks, after which one can request to make it into a three- or five-year order. I do not recommend this, at least in terms of doing an intervention. Interventions are all about short-term actions.

If the person fails to obey the restraining order, it's an *infraction*–not even a misdemeanor–although if he continues to violate the order, he can get into trouble. The benefit of a TRO is that it can be *the* deciding factor in getting somebody to go to treatment.

Generally, the order will be served either by a deputy sheriff, or someone over 18 other than the complainant, at which point the person will be given 15 to 30 minutes to collect his things and leave. He will then be told if he comes back he will be in violation of the order.

Once the person has left the premises, he may be furious. *This is to be expected.* It's important that you not take a punitive or condescending stance toward him once you get the TRO. You should also be aware that the TRO may restrict *you* as well as him, and prohibit you from speaking with the person named in the order, but with thorough planning beforehand this *can* all work in your favor.

Finally, keep what you're planning secret if possible. A restraining order can give you the upper hand, but if you threaten the addict with it before it's granted, thereby giving him time to make other arrangements, you may give up the advantage.

Vigilantism

Some people believe that if they could just get their loved one's dealers busted, their loved one will be more likely to cooperate. What is more likely to happen is the exact opposite. If there is some benefit, I don't know what it would be; I cannot speak to every single possibility, but I can speak to what happens most of the time.

There are two myths that are usually the culprits when family members make it their mission to have dealers arrested, aside from the anger and negative emotions involved.

The first false belief is that by stopping the supply from a dealer, one can stop the supply to the addict. If, however, you think that having a dealer or two busted is going to motivate your loved one to go to a program, you are not only underestimating the power of addiction, you are probably setting yourself up to have a much larger problem on your hands.

When the addict finds out what you've done—*and he will*—he's going to be so upset with you there will be *less* of a chance of getting him into a program. While you may get some emotional payoff by trying to get people arrested, and even feel like you're accomplishing something, all you're doing is creating an unnecessary fight. I'm not saying this is true in every single case and, obviously, if I am doing an intervention and feel that having a person's dealer busted is a good tactical decision *and* there's a way to do it that makes sense, I'll be the first to move that agenda forward. My warning is against doing it out of vengeance, entertaining the fantasy that you're going to show up with the police in tow and somehow intimidate the addict into submission, or leave him without alternatives. But be careful what you ask for—you just might get it.

The second false belief is that law enforcement is going to arrest someone simply because you tell them he's using or selling drugs. *Not true*. Police don't go kicking in doors just because someone gives them a "hot tip." Police get tips *all the time;* they hear from freaked-out parents, jealous boyfriends, and vengeful wives.

I once had a case where the father had tracked his son using a GPS system. The father was quite smug about what he had accomplished. He showed me a map of all the stops his son had made when he was out using. He pointed to various spots where he knew his son had bought drugs. In his mind, he was planning a sweep of these locations (I'm not exactly certain how—maybe wearing leotards and a cape). The fact was that the son was alienated from his father and hadn't spoken to him in some time *because* of his vigilante behavior. If your goal is to get someone into treatment, then focus on *that* and not on being a DEA vigilante. It won't help.

Medical

Ahhh, the irony of using medical issues as a reason *not* to go into treatment.

Trust me, unless there is a medical emergency requiring immediate hospitalization, the best place for an addict who needs medical attention in addition to rehab is *in* the treatment facility.

All treatment facilities have access to doctors, and their staff *expects* new clients to have medical issues. In fact, it's far more unusual that a person would start treatment in perfect health. Some of those aches and pains will be excuses, but if the illness is real, it is *still* better dealt with by doctors *at the treatment center.* Also, a person is better able to recover if he is clean and his body is not dealing with the ongoing onslaught of chemicals or alcohol.

When I was an addict, I used "illness" to avoid school, work, or when I just wanted to lie around drinking or doing nothing at all.

To resist going to a treatment center where one will get cleaned up *and* get medical attention *because* of medical reasons doesn't make any sense.

Whether the illness is real is beside the point of an intervention. The treatment center is where the addict or alcoholic needs to be.

Functioning Alcoholics?

"Once during Prohibition, I was forced to live on

nothing but food and water."

~ W.C. Fields

Whoever coined the phrase "functioning alcoholic" had to be a drinker. The term conjures up an image of someone who holds down a career while, at the same time, saturating himself with a central nervous system depressant. To anyone who says that person is "functioning," I have to ask, "... as *what?*" If happiness and a life well-lived are not a priority, then sure.

Think of a heroin addict. Would you consider that person to be a *functioning* drug addict as long as he's employed?

When I hear the term "functioning alcoholic," I hear a justification by the alcoholic and/or his family to do nothing about an obvious problem. "He maintains his job and *says* he's happy, so the rest of us don't need to do anything about the fact that he's drinking himself to death." This kind of statement will never be anything other than an excuse, no matter how many people you get to agree with you.

Drinking enough to justify being labeled as an alcoholic indicates somebody who is deeply disturbed or depressed, and the fact that he has a job while doing it doesn't make it less of a problem.

If you care about your loved one's happiness and well-being, stop letting him or her use a job or career as a defense against handling a very real problem.

I have done interventions for all classes and kinds of people and addiction knows no barriers of money, education, gender or ethnicity.

There is no real quality of life if one is only able to hold a job but is depressed or isolated from the pleasures of living. This is not *truly living*.

When did our standards drop so low as to believe for a single second that functioning is a measure of survival *only* since we are capable of so much more?

What happened to fulfillment? What happened to *thriving*?

Those People

"Do not judge and you will never be mistaken."

~ *Jean Jacques Rousseau*

When most people think of crack cocaine, they think of scary people in some scary neighborhood in some scary part of the world.

"Crack addict" conjures up images of inner city gang violence or a misfit slithering through the subway. One thinks of shady deals in dark alleys, people shooting each other, cops busting through gated doors.

When I used to buy drugs, my dealers hung out on 98th and D Streets in Oakland. I bought crack on the outskirts of New York's Central Park and in the projects of the Ninth Ward in New Orleans. These are the sorts of places you'd *expect* to find crack, but I'd like to share something with you: I was working with a family in Kentucky, a classic middle American family, owners of some of the most beautiful and fertile farmland in the world. They had "old" money; their farms were large and had been in their family for generations.

William was 70 years old, had two hundred head of cattle, other signs of prosperity, and his life was torn apart by drinking and his recently acquired *crack* habit.

William wasn't from a scary neighborhood or a low-income family. He wasn't "ethnic." He was about as middle-class-white-American as anybody can get–and his story is in this book.

I did an intervention in Alliance, Nebraska which offered a similar lesson.

Alliance is a whistle stop, a small railroad depot, sixty miles from the nearest town. I was sitting with the addict's grandmother talking to her about her grandson's cocaine addiction. He was freebasing, the equivalent of smoking crack. She said something to me that I would continue to hear on a regular basis, no matter where my work took me. "I know that drugs are an epidemic everywhere," she said, " but did you know that Alliance, Nebraska is the *worst* area for cocaine? It's true, the sheriff told me that." So here I am looking around at this white bread family from a podunk town in the middle of nowhere, and this woman is telling me "it's the worst area in the country for cocaine."

Whatever city I am working in is "the worst area for _____."

"Oakland is the worst area for heroin."

"Tennessee is the worst area for prescription drugs."

"New York for crack... Montana for meth..."

Pick a city, pick a demographic, pick a drug.

Drug abuse is *everywhere* and it can affect anyone at any time, especially when someone believes he is too smart, too rich, or immune from the possibility that it will happen to him.

I've used drugs in the suburbs of the richest areas in the United States, and in the most remote farmland. I've bought dope in the worst areas of New York and in the bucolic foothills of the Sierra Nevada. *It doesn't make any difference where you live, how much money you have or what your bloodline is.* People can *pretend* it does because they drink single malt scotch and not Ripple, or because their opiates are prescribed by pain management clinics, or because they have a medical marijuana card.

If you think that you or your family is somehow exempt from the effects or temptation of drug addiction, *think again.*

82

I have heard the term "those people" spoken aloud and seen it behind the silent, condescending scorn some people seem to have when it comes to addicts. I think to myself, *You could be next.*

One day you might find yourself justifying a drink or two or three or four, maybe an extra pain pill (or three or four or six) to numb some part of life. Over weeks, months or years you might find yourself to *be* one of "those people."

But—know this—you'll be in good company:

Howard Hughes: One of the fathers of modern aviation was also a lifelong addict to codeine and valium.

Johnny Cash: Legendary singer and songwriter, his addiction to amphetamines and barbiturates was just as legendary.

Stephen King: Upon finding him passed out at his desk in a pool of his own blood and vomit, King's wife reportedly threatened to take his children with her and leave him if he did not stop using cocaine and drinking. With the threat of losing his family looming over his head, King cleaned up and, with his wife's help, slowly began writing again. Sober, he authored some of his most compelling works including *Hearts in Atlantis* and *The Green Mile.*

Dr. William Halstead: Known as the father of modern surgery, Dr. Halstead pioneered the mastectomy and the use of rubber gloves in the operating room. He also worked on developing cocaine as a stable anesthesia. Between surgeries he used cocaine, as well as morphine.

Dr. Sigmund Freud: Known as the father of psychoanalysis, Freud wrote extensively about his use of cocaine which he said made him feel super-human, at one point publishing a well-regarded paper called *Über Coca,* "a song of praise to this magical substance."

Aaron Sorkin: Sorkin wrote *The West Wing, A Few Good Men, Charlie Wilson's War* and *The Social Network,* but he may be best known for saying, "The hardest thing I do every day is not to take cocaine."

Charlie "Yardbird" Parker: Partner to Dizzy Gillespie and father of the style of jazz we now know as "Bebop." He died at the age of 34 as the result of alcoholism and opiate addiction.

Betty Ford: This first lady's recovery from alcoholism is legendary, largely because she did so much to fight alcoholism and drug addiction, including providing comprehensive recovery at the renowned Betty Ford Clinic.

Some of our *best people* become addicts and alcoholics, and you never know what a down-and-out addict or alcoholic might do with his or her recovery! Once he's cleaned up and back in good shape again, your loved one could very well use his current situation to help others.

Many among us have taken walks on the "lower roads" of addiction or alcoholism and later have become an influence for good. In fact, I can't think of a single intervention I have done that wasn't to help someone who was too smart for his own good.

The Enabler

"The greatest mistake you can make in life is to be continually fearing you will make one."
~ Elbert Hubbard

"Enabler" is one of the most misused words in the lexicon of addiction.

The term "enabling" is often hurled at parents as an accusation of helping facilitate someone, typically a son or daughter, along a path of drug-addicted self-destruction. To me, however, it's *absurd* to suggest that a mother or father would be a willing accessory to their child's addiction. Parents don't "help" destroy their children.

Many parents reading this may have been accused of enabling. If that has happened to you, I am sorry the people you love are accusing you of deliberately worsening your loved one's condition. A good parent would never do that—not in a million years. What I see is that you are caught in a struggle between love and fear, and it's difficult to know whether you are helping or hurting.

Let us say you are providing financial support, like paying the rent, for your drug-addicted or alcoholic son or daughter, knowing that he or she would otherwise be homeless. Your other children, and maybe your spouse, are telling you, "You've got to stop *enabling* _____. You have to cut him off, let him hit 'bottom,' otherwise he'll never get help."

But, you have your own reality on the subject.

You're thinking, "Okay, so here's my child whom I brought into this world to love, raise and protect. Now he's using drugs and isn't able to take care of himself. My other children are loving, but resentful. I know they are trying to solve the problem by telling me to cut him off, but cutting him off does not solve the problem nor is there any guarantee that by doing so I won't make the problem worse."

It's the school of thought that says, "If we don't support him, he'll have to give in and agree to go to the program." The *tough love* approach.

You are running scenarios through your head that keep you in a state of fear about what this might mean. In one sense, what you're being told is logical. You can see how providing the financial means for your child to get drugs or alcohol is destructive. On the other hand, you're afraid that if you cut all ties with your dysfunctional son or daughter, the dysfunction will not only continue but you might lose touch with him and put his life in danger. It's a textbook damned-if-you-do, damned-if-you-don't scenario.

Handing an addict cash might be just what people describe–like handing him a loaded gun. However, you may feel that cutting him off carries no guarantee your child will seek help and is equally scary in many ways.

Just because one scenario makes sense to some of the family does not mean the person supplying the support will agree.

You may see your addicted child as too prideful or bull-headed to ever *submit*, so you're convinced that if you cut him off, he'll become more criminal, more addicted or, worse, may die; and his death will be your fault. That's a terrible position to be in. Talk about being stuck between a rock and a hard place.

There is a way I believe it can be handled.

Having established that "helping an addict maintain his addiction" is not "enabling" but that the so-called "enabler" is trying to prevent further harm to the addict, what is the missing piece?

Each person in an intervention needs solutions that make sense to him. If cutting off resources is a necessary step, listen to the person providing the resources and try to reconcile his or her fears. Suggest that the disconnection doesn't need to be permanent but is a tactical move. Don't be aggressive or condescending in your arguments, which is often the case when people talk about other members of their family being enablers. It's important to really *listen* and find a path that can be agreed upon and followed—one that is realistic.

And for you parents out there, keep an open mind especially to the fact that abrupt and sudden change can be an effective way to bring about permanent, broader change. If you've been providing support to a child, and he or she has not sought help, try to think of what you would require in order to stop providing resources to the addict, and then put your thoughts on the table. If you want things to turn out differently, you'll need to do things differently.

Pretend you own a ranch. On your ranch is a lake. You own a cow that drinks from the lake. One year the lake becomes contaminated. You decide to create a new lake for her to drink from. However your cow prefers the water from the contaminated pond. She doesn't have to move very far and so refuses to walk to the new one. She moos loudly and digs in her hooves, eyeing you angrily for trying to force her to move. The answer is simple. *Fence off the contaminated lake.* The cow will moo and moo, but eventually she must drink from the new lake.

Psychiatric Evaluations

"It's easy to get a thousand prescriptions but hard to find one remedy."

~ Chinese Proverb

Addicts and alcoholics are well-acquainted with psychoses, anxiety, and depression. Not only do drugs and alcohol affect the mind, but the efforts associated with their procurement—like lying, theft and other immoral or unethical acts—can have long-term and devastating effects on a person's conscience, self-esteem and self-worth.

Alcohol is classified as a central nervous system depressant, whereas marijuana and Hydrocodone (OxyContin) are psychoactive and can alter perception, mood, or consciousness. Hydrocodone is also an analgesic, a drug that causes the loss of the ability to feel pain while conscious.

Drug-induced psychoses can be caused by a combination of things including psychoactive drugs, street drugs, vitamin and mineral deficiencies resulting from their use combined with dehydration and food and sleep deprivation.

Reversing and repairing this begins by *removing* the drugs or alcohol and then returning the person to a state of physical health. Once the person's health returns and he can operate cognitively again, he can begin addressing and resolving the events that caused the anxiety, guilt, and depression that he sought to relieve by drinking or taking drugs in the first place.

Psychiatric Evaluations and Psychoactive Meds

Count me as a cynic when it comes to psychoactive medications.

89

Know also that many of the families I work with share my cynicism.

Because of their behavior, people who are using drugs or drinking are often subject to psychiatric evaluations, which in turn lead to the prescribing of psychoactive drugs. The unfortunate irony is that most psychoactive drugs have side effects that can be worse than the ailments they are intended to abate. In addition to this, *any diagnosis of a person using drugs or drinking heavily will indicate <u>a drugged</u> state of mind which is, by definition, unbalanced.*

If you've ever drunk alcohol or smoked pot over a long period of time then you know what I'm talking about. Eventually, your overall state of mind becomes more depressed than you would be otherwise. If a psychiatrist were to ask you why you were depressed and you didn't identify it with the drugs or alcohol, indicating instead that you didn't know, it's likely you'd walk out of that office with at least one prescription.

On one hand, you have street drugs, which we use in order to avoid having to deal with our feelings. On the other, you have psychoactive drugs, which we use in order to avoid having to deal with our feelings only they don't get us arrested. The catch is that many of the drugs advertised do not create a balanced state of mind, quite the contrary in fact. Many come with black box warnings.

Here is a list of "possible side effects" for a popular antidepressant *currently* advertised on TV. I copied this list right from the drug manufacturer's website:

"Neuroleptic Malignant Syndrome, characterized by fever, muscular rigidity, altered mental state, autonomic dysfunction and occurs shortly after the initiation of neuroleptic treatment, or after dose increases, *increased chance of suicide*, Tardive Dyskinesia, uncontrollable movements

90

of the face and tongue; cognitive impairment, effects on a person's judgment; increased risk of stroke; decreases in white blood cells; seizures; decreased blood pressure; difficulty swallowing; excessive weight gain."

Some antidepressants even indicate *"an increase in homicidal tendencies..."*

Today, nearly 30 years after the introduction of Prozac (the most profitable drug in the world), people who once flocked to the promise of emotional well-being in pill form have seen too much evidence to the contrary and realize that the neurological effects of long-term psychoactive drug use can become permanent.

While I appreciate and respect the fact that for some, medication may be necessary where an actual medical disorder exists, but honor, integrity, honesty, morality courage or happiness will never result from taking a pill. Once lost to addiction, those things take hard work to regain.

In my experience, when a person has faced the problems that he needs to face and does the work necessary to free himself, his depression, anxiety, and manic behavior will subside or vanish and will be replaced by an increased sense of personal responsibility and self-worth, a true life. This is the purpose of rehabilitation.

My advice: find a program that addresses the *why* behind anxiety and depression. The result will be someone able to face life and feel happiness for having done so.

Can We Get Our Loved One *Committed?*

Your loved one may be hearing voices, be afraid of the Illuminati, hidden cameras, FBI agents hiding in the trees, or even you. He may be seeing bugs coming after him. He may be violent, completely out of control, afraid of shadow people or convinced of a conspiracy against him. You may look at these behaviors and think, "He needs to be in a *mental hospital*, not a treatment center!"

I have some personal experience with this which I hope can provide you with some insight.

Before I went to treatment, I had sequestered myself to an RV where I smoked bath salts, a modern street drug. I began seeing things, really *horrible* things. I saw bugs crawling along the floor coming after me. I literally sat in the same spot in the RV, terrified, for about 36 hours straight. When I rubbed my eyes, tiny segmented worms came out: This wasn't like the hallucinations I had when I was younger and tripped on acid or mushrooms. *Those* hallucinations were fun and colorful. *These* seemed real and were terrifying. When I looked carefully under the light at the worms coming out of my eyes, they wriggled on my fingertips.

I remember one day I smoked some of the bath salts and then went to a grocery store where I bought a roast chicken. When I brought it home, I was certain there was a large, mutated parasite inside the container. I looked at the chicken closely; it didn't seem *right* to me. I concluded that it must have been grown in a laboratory. I then concluded that the slug (which turned out to be a piece of chicken skin) was a parasite that had been grown in the lab along with the chicken. I decided it would be a good idea to text my mother. I sent her pictures of the "parasite" which I had named Ruth. My mother texted me back that she hoped I would get help.

I was furious that she didn't believe me. I explained to her that the recall and euthanasia of chickens that had appeared in the news recently was actually a cover story to hide the fact the chickens were now grown in laboratories. I further explained that Ruth was probably a parasite that had accidentally made it into the laboratory and was artificially "overgrown" along with the chicken.

You can imagine what my family and friends were thinking at this point.

When I told my best friend about Ruth and what my mother had said, she told me I should avoid going to the hospital. She didn't say it, but she was thinking they might have me committed.

Her attitude at the time neatly summarizes the kind of viewpoint I wish every family could have when it comes to drug-induced psychoses: Unless the person is a danger to himself or others, and if you know or strongly suspect that drug abuse is behind the aberrant behavior, *avoid psychiatric hospitals;* continue with your efforts to get the person into a treatment center.

As I write this, I am greatly relieved that my family and those close to me knew that these hallucinations were drug related and took immediate steps to get me into treatment.

My mother, who lived 500 miles away, asked a drug counselor and my brother to come to see me. The next day I checked into a holistic detox center, one that does *not* use psychiatric medications.

It took me a few days to come in for a landing. Once my hallucinations went away, I slept for several days. The staff quietly kept an eye on me, making sure I was eating good, healthful food, taking vitamins, getting a little exercise and, most of all, plenty of rest. After about three weeks in the program, I began to feel and act like myself again.

If my family had committed me to a mental institution, or the ER doctor had ordered a 72-hour hold, I'm certain I would have been assessed with schizophrenia, paranoid psychosis, mania or any number of other conditions which would have justified a cocktail of psychiatric medications. I would probably have ended up sequestered to at-home care with my emotions bottled up in my prescriptions.

5150's and the 48/72-Hour Hold

In giving you this information I am _not_ suggesting deliberately getting someone locked up in a psychiatric ward as an intervention strategy but, since addicts get themselves locked up all on their own, if your loved one _does_ end up in a psych ward, what you're about to read may prove useful.

"5150" refers to somebody who is involuntarily confined to a psychiatric hospital because he is deemed to be a danger to himself or others. The term originally referred to a section of the California Welfare and Institutions Code but is now commonly used to mean anybody who gets locked up in a psych ward as a protective measure.

The first thing to understand about a temporary psychiatric hold is that it is _temporary_. In some states, it's for 72 hours; in others, the hold is for 48. These are the _maximum_ number of hours an adult can be held involuntarily without being formally committed by a judge. This means that if your loved one is taken to a psych ward on a temporary hold and you already have a treatment program in place, you must act quickly; _more importantly,_ you must work _smart; you must not work in a panicked state if you are to use the situation to your advantage._

Unless you know which program your loved one is going to, a psychiatric hold can produce a crisis because the clock will suddenly start running.

Don't continue unprepared: Do your research about treatment programs *before* your addict does something that results in him or her being locked up on a psychiatric hold and that 72- or 48-hour clock starts ticking. Otherwise, you might feel forced to choose a program and end up with one that isn't a good fit for your loved one, and then end up right back where you started. This is why *today* is the day to do your research about a treatment program so if things get dicey, you'll be ready.

In terms of getting somebody released from a psychiatric ward directly to a treatment program, there are a few things to know about how to make that happen.

First, get a letter from the treatment center outlining their program. Be sure it says they address "dual diagnosis" cases. The letter should speak to the nature of the program, the length of the program, the level of observation and supervision, and so on. These are the factors that will be important to the psychiatrist adjudicating your loved one's case. Take the letter to the psych ward and, if possible, present it to the *attending psychiatrist*, not his junior or a duty nurse. Make your case in person.

Make sure the doctor understands that your loved one ended up in the psych ward as the result of his alcohol or drug abuse and that transferring him directly to the treatment program will be in his best interest. Ideally, you would also have somebody from the program there with you when you make this request. That way the doctor is assured of the person's arrival at the program. If the psychiatrist is insisting that the person be medicated, don't argue. That can be handled at the treatment center. Your loved one can be weaned off whatever they put him on, as appropriate.

Remember that a 72- or 48-hour hold is the *maximum* amount of time the person can be held, not the minimum. In other words, the person being held could be released in one, eight, or twelve hours. It's up to the attending physician to decide if the person continues to present a danger to himself or others. But again, don't let this cause you to get into a frenzy. Do your best to keep a level head, and *work smart.*

Finally, don't make the mistake of equating a psychiatric hospital with a drug or alcohol rehabilitation program. Psychiatric hospitals are *by definition* for people who are psychotic and, while the behavior of the person you love may fall into this category now, *drug-induced* psychosis, paranoia, and mania are more appropriately addressed in a good drug treatment program where the person can get *away* from the drugs and regain his sanity.

Part III

Strategy & Tactics

Planning

"A goal without a plan is just a wish."

~ Antoine de Saint-Exupery

When people ask me how I succeed, I tell them I do a lot of planning, and then I plan some more.

Preparation is the best way to prevent sudden upheavals or panic and the best way to promote certainty within the family about what to do at any given time.

Most interventions that fail do so due to a lack of planning. Families tend to be perfectly ready to initiate a meeting and make the offer of help, but when a peaceful intervention turns into a Wes Craven movie, many families find themselves without a solid contingency plan, unable to control the situation–all because of a lack of planning.

Planning and the ability to abandon or create new plans as you go may be the single most important aspect of a successful intervention.

It's like prepping a house to be painted. If you go into it thinking that preparation doesn't matter as much as getting a few gallons of paint on the walls, you soon realize, as the paint peels after the first rain, that you should have taken the time to put on a coat of primer instead of rushing to paint.

Pushing through an intervention in an emotionally charged state is fine, even expected, but *it's not an excuse to be reckless or unprepared.*

Ninety-nine percent of intervention disasters are caused by families rushing in, bypassing preparation in favor of "getting it over with." When all hell breaks loose, those families have no idea what to do.

They pull their hair out, blaming each other or the overwhelming power of the addiction when the problem was simpler than that...*it was a lack of planning.*

Part of winning is staying in one piece so that if something happens, you can continue the race. In preparing for an intervention, instead of being afraid that a crisis will occur, *plan* for it to occur and how you'll handle it. Take the time to be meticulous and thorough; you will *never* regret the time spent doing it. You may not use every contingency you plan for, but if you need them they'll be there.

Here's an example: If you think there's even a slight chance the addict will walk out of the meeting, then you need to come up with a scenario where you *plan* for him to walk out. This means assigning someone to go after him, deciding exactly what that person will say to bring him back, figuring out how far to let the addict go if it gets confrontational, and planning where and when the family will regroup afterward. This way, if the addict does walk out, *you have a plan.*

Because you *know* how the addict typically behaves, you can probably predict how he or she will react to certain things. If you offer the addict help for his heroin addiction for instance, you might guess correctly that he will accuse his mother of having an addiction to pain pills, or accuse his sister of getting him started on the drug, or blame his entire family for not making the offer the right way. *These are common situations.* On the one hand, you have a loved one who is losing his life to drugs or alcohol and, on the other, a hypocrisy in the family he will use as an excuse to refuse help. One of the best ways I've found to handle this is to place the hypocrisy out in the open before he does. This denies him the opportunity to weaponize it.

If, for example, the father drinks a lot, and it's likely that the addict will use this as an argument against going to treatment by accusing his dad of being a hypocrite, a possible solution is for the father to include in his letter to the addict a part where he accepts responsibility for his drinking. He can acknowledge that he understands it's unfair to expect the addict to "do as I say, not as I do." Then the father states his willingness to address his own demons while his son gets help with his. He might even apologize for not being a better example to his son. It is important to understand that you're *not* handling the fathers drinking in doing this. *You are handling the potential for the addict to use it as an objection.* By naming it and taking responsibility for it before he uses it as an accusation, you deny *him* the chance to use it.

Then, in your planning, move on to the next thing you feel <u>might</u> happen, even if you feel it won't. Plan for it to happen, and lay out what your solution will be. In the end, you may have ten contingency plans that you've spent an extra hour or two mapping out so, even if only *one* of them happens you'll be ready for it and won't be set back days because of it. Most importantly, the intervention will not have failed because of it.

As simple as thorough planning sounds, *it is the most overlooked aspect of interventions.*

I'm always hearing families tell me that their efforts at an intervention failed, but when they fill me in on the details, the problem is either a failure to plan *or* their having given up too soon.

Secrets and Lies

"I trust everybody. I just don't trust the devil inside them."

~ Troy Kennedy

As you and your team talk about doing the intervention, some of you might be tempted to tell the addict about it.

Don't.

Letting the addict know what's going on is unwise and will make your intervention many times more difficult. No matter how uncomfortable you may feel about keeping it secret, *it's better for the person you are trying to help*. It's something surprise parties and interventions have in common. If you want it to be a success, *keep it a secret*.

A true friend or family member must accept the fact that you don't want to do *anything* that will lessen the chances for success.

The most common reason for the discomfort associated with keeping the intervention secret is a fear of how the addict will react when the offer of help is made. Imagining accusations of betrayal can make someone in the family want to be *the good guy* and confide in the addict, rationalizing that the addict will appreciate the gesture and want to avoid the intervention by agreeing to go to the program, or something along those lines. That is a perfectly normal reaction–the natural desire to avoid confrontation. At a certain point, however, you have to stop trying to be the addict's confidante and, instead, do what will save his life.

Accept the fact the addict is going to accuse you of keeping a secret and betraying his trust.

That's a definite possibility so you need to plan for that to take place and have an appropriate response.

Once the big secret is known, the easiest thing to say is: "Yes, it's true. We have kept this from you because we wanted to be prepared. We wanted the offer to be right. We knew this wasn't something you would necessarily want to do, so we took the time to choose a program we felt would be most appealing to you and which could also bring you back to us. *You mean too much to us for us to have done it any other way.*"

If the addict still accuses you of betrayal, respond by telling him that true betrayal would be to do nothing, allowing him to continue the way he is—*that* would be a betrayal. Accusations of betrayal by the addict will likely continue despite what you say, but don't let that deter you. Even though it may not seem like it, embroiled addicts hear what you're saying.

If you need someone to be involved but can't trust him to keep a secret, make your plans in advance and bring him in at the very last minute so he doesn't have time to spill the beans.

If your plans are discovered beforehand, *don't panic.* You might get more open criticism from the addict, and certainly earlier than planned. You might have to spend more time convincing him to meet with you, but nothing else changes. It's just easier to conduct an intervention if you can stay comfortably ahead of the addict.

No matter what the addict may say, you can never be wrong for trying to help or for keeping things secret as part of an overall plan to save that person's life. As I said, if you want to betray the addict, divulging your plans too early will do just that.

The Use of Deception

An intervention is one of the most loving things a family can do, but it may require calculated deception in order to get the job done.

For anybody who has lost a loved one to alcoholism or addiction or recovered one, this is an easy question to answer.

Within reason, you need to do what you need to do to get the job done. As an example, I need to get an addict to agree to go to treatment but telling him I am an interventionist up front is not always advisable, so I'm often introduced as someone the family happened to come across over the course of researching programs. Sometimes I tell the addict I'm there as a negotiator to help facilitate things, both are essentially true. If the addict asks me if I'm an interventionist, I'll tell him I've been involved in a few interventions and his family offered to throw me a little something and cover my expenses to come out and help get things going.

It may seem like a fine point but it's important that the addict doesn't feel threatened. By putting myself on the back burner and not coming off as the person in charge, the addict perceives the ultimatums and the *force* behind the intervention as coming from the family, not from me. The addict can still feel safe talking to me and the treatment center can be made to seem like a refuge, not a prison.

While the use of deception may be justifiable when it comes to *strategy*, you do need to be careful about being dishonest in describing the program. It's alright to exaggerate a little in terms of the amenities: If you can make the satellite TV sounds like a good place to hang out or watch football on the weekends, go ahead. If you want to make the facility's gym sound like the perfect place for the addict to get his health back, fine.

You could probably even make the whole time there sound like a vacation for him from the family. Do not, however, tell your loved one that there is a lake if there isn't one or that they have a hot tub if they don't. That's "bad pool." If and when your loved one goes there and discovers your lies, he might reject the program on sight, get paranoid about you and the facility, and wonder when the other shoe is going to drop.

In conclusion, be careful how you use deception. Don't be afraid of it—just be smart about it. And don't use deception out of anger or as a reaction if you can help it; only use it if you know it will help your cause.

Brute, Emotional Force

"He who angers you conquers you."

~ Elizabeth Kenny

When I see an addict ripping into his mother in response to an offer of help, I see an addict trying to control the outcome of the argument using brute, emotional force. I see someone who doesn't want to do something, improvising ways to get out of it and, if the other person allows it to affect him or her, the addict may succeed. By driving his family into a state of apathy, panic or hopelessness, the addict hopes to force them to give up.

Interventions are difficult, emotional times. The addict will try to capitalize on this, pitting family members against each other, lashing out, screaming bloody murder or quietly, *yet convincingly*, tell you he'll never go to treatment.

If you find this taking place, it's important you recognize it for what it is: an *effort at control,* an effort at making you wrong, making the offer wrong, making the program wrong and ultimately, avoiding going.

The addict may go to extremes with threats of suicide or promises to never speak to anyone again, to commit crimes or otherwise try to force his family to believe that continuing with the intervention is more dangerous than not. You may become exhausted and frazzled. *You may want to give up.* You may want to fall into a dark hole and forget about all of it. Remember—*this is how addicts keep themselves and their families imprisoned.*

Knowing what I'm telling you is one thing, but keep in mind that *you will get nowhere if you begin accusing the addict of using crisis as a means of control.* First, it is more of an automatic response than something premeditated, and second, the only result of being confrontational about it will be a fight. So absorb what I'm telling you so you can see the addict's behavior for what it is, but do not throw it in the addict's face. That will not get you anywhere.

Destruction of Property

During times of emotional upheaval, the addict may engage in the destruction of property. This can range anywhere from throwing a plate across the room, to punching a hole in the wall, to driving a car into the fence. I've had all of these things happen on multiple occasions.

Like yelling and screaming, destroying property is another effort at control, only at a higher magnitude. It is one of the ways an addict who has his back up against a wall, tries to throw people off balance.

It's ironic if you think about it. This kind of behavior is exactly *why* the person needs to go to treatment in the first place

Whether the destruction of property is a regular occurrence or the addict is engaging in it for the very first time, the same rules apply when it comes to doing an intervention. Some may even say it's an advantage to be dealing with someone who acts out a lot because you have something to shut down.

Do not tolerate destruction of property. You cannot and *must not* allow it to continue. I'm talking close to zero tolerance. By shutting down the behavior, you transmit a very clear message to the addict that it's not business as usual.

If the person punches a hole in the wall and then calms down and wants to talk about going to the program—then fine, you probably don't need to call the police. If however he punches a hole in the wall, slams the door, kicks a window out and makes no indication that he's going to stop, *dial 9-1-1. Shut it down.*

I can't promise anything but, in most cases, the police will not want to take anyone to jail if the disturbance can be worked out. Destruction of property is illegal, but in most cases it's up to the property owner to press charges. The exception would be a person who already has a warrant out for his arrest but, even in that case, you still need to follow through if the addict is using that as a way of arguing you out of calling the police. "If you call the police, I'll get arrested." And then he's back to punching holes in walls. This is being held hostage to violence and, for those of you who have lived with this for a time, I sympathize with how difficult it can be to take this step even though logic tells you it's the right thing to do.

If you have a friend who tells you someone he loves is using drugs or drinking, and, in addition to the addiction, is throwing fits of violence and destroying property, making threats, what would you tell your friend to do? Would you advise him to allow all of this to continue simply because he's afraid? Or would you tell him he can't go on allowing the person he loves to control the relationship with violence?

Ask yourself, who *are* you in this story? The one who allows the addict to continue, or the one who gets him to stop and puts an end to it? It's up to *you* to create *your* storyline.

Crisis

Webster's Dictionary defines a crisis as:

1. *a. A paroxysmal attack of pain, distress, or disordered function. b. An emotionally significant event or radical change of status in a person's life.*
2. *a. An unstable or crucial time or state-of-affairs in which a decisive change is impending, especially one with the distinct possibility of a highly undesirable outcome. b. A situation that has reached a critical phase.*

It can be difficult for a family member, especially a non-addict, to understand why crises are such a regular occurrence in an addict's life.

The purpose of this chapter is to help family members understand that crises and turmoil in an addict's life are his means of controlling and manipulating those around him. It's important to realize that crisis is a way of life for an addict, not something directed at you personally, so don't panic when things erupt!

Because crisis is such an integral part of his life and he is such a slave to it, manipulating situations through chaos becomes his normal way to survive. An addict's family is often estranged, and he may have no job, no home, no support system.

To him, there is a reality behind each crisis:

How am I going to pay for my next bag (or bottle)?

What excuse am I going to use for missing work?

How long have I been up/asleep?

How am I going to explain having missed Thanksgiving, Christmas or a birthday, etc.?

What am I going to do about the rent, car payment, phone bill, student loan?

The way addicts operate can make their brand of chaos seem premeditated and disturbingly well thought out, but this is not usually the case. In fact, an addict's life is in such disarray that he must constantly figure his way around the next obstacle.

Families often see *each* crisis as a *new problem* to deal with when, in fact, the individual problems are simply the continuation of addiction as it worsens. When you step back and look at the addict's history, you will see a steady decline in the person's life, each major crisis a flagstone in a downward-spiraling path. It's actually something you can take comfort in because what you're seeing is the progression of the condition, the same condition that, to a greater or lesser degree, every addict or alcoholic is in. It's not unique to your loved one, and it is not a question of degraded moral fiber which is why your addict is in such conflict with himself and the world. Take hope in the fact that without real moral fiber and ethics, your loved one would not be in any conflict at all. So, in this sense, severe personal conflict is a good sign.

However, when the intervention is perceived to be out of control, family members are much more likely to throw in the towel and give up, and that is precisely why addicts spend such inordinate amounts of energy generating out-of-control scenarios.

Effective interventions are the result of people staying calm and keeping the game moving, *regardless* of what occurs.

Panic

When you panic, you lose control of the situation. When you panic, the situation controls *you*.

When a crisis hits, the key is to *stay calm* and remind yourself that the crisis is part of the condition you are there to solve.

It may be the most important piece of advice in this book: Do not allow yourself to fall into panic due to the dramatic unwillingness of the addict.

Hopelessness

1. *Without hope [a hopeless prisoner].*
2. *Causing one to lose hope; discouraging [a hopeless situation].*

Practicing addicts try to destroy interventions by creating feelings of hopelessness in those around them—parents, spouses and others close to them. It is a simple yet powerful mechanism that is not difficult to observe if you look for it. If you see it, you can plan for it. If you plan for it, you can stay ahead of it. If you can stay ahead of it, you will have a greater level of control.

Here are some examples of how an addict creates hopelessness:

"No matter WHAT you say or do, I'll NEVER go to treatment!!"

"I'm going to KILL myself if you make me go!!"

"I can do it on my OWN!!"

"I have THINGS TO DO!!"

"I WOULD have gone, but this intervention sure changed *that*!!"

"If you make me go, I'll just leave once I get there!!"

...ad nauseum.

Every one of these statements and the way they are delivered have but one clear purpose: to create hopelessness and fear in those who are trying to help, thereby getting them to give up or change direction.

The entrenched addict makes his family wrong for trying to help.

114

Word by word, crisis by crisis, explosion by explosion, the using and stuck addict makes you WRONG, WRONG, *WRONG* for having the *nerve* to have any hope at all.

This is *not* malicious. The addict is not thinking, "I'm going to make my family feel hopeless." What he's doing is more of an automatic response to a perceived threat. The reason he responds the *way* he does is because it has worked for him in the past. If creating a crisis throws people off guard, makes them second-guess what they're doing and instills doubt, then what would you *expect* an addict to do during an intervention? As I said, the best response is to expect it, stay calm and keep the offer and ultimatums moving. In other words, don't let a little fire stop the train.

The intensity of an addict's crises will increase in proportion to how threatened he feels. During the intervention, for example, he is forced to face something he does not want to do, something that is incredibly difficult, so he will play whatever card he believes will make things go his way. No big mystery here.

So how do you succeed in the face of vehement resistance?

Expect it. Plan for it.

You should *expect* and *plan* for a crisis to occur, if not volley after volley of them. You need to be mentally prepared so when crises occur you can maintain a level head and not panic. During an intervention, crises are not so much the enemy as is *panicking* in response to them.

Keep in mind that a crisis is not necessarily something loud and flammable. A crisis is whatever the addict can do that creates a certain kind of reaction in others.

In other words, if isolating himself, not answering his phone and sinking into a pit of despair causes others to stop in their tracks and second-guess what they're doing, then that's what he'll do. I'm talking about anything that causes critical players to panic, become hopeless or fearful, doubt themselves, and otherwise become emotionally stopped.

Expecting the addict will have more than one crisis–and allowing enough time to handle each one–is something that distinguishes effective interventions from those which fail.

Mainstream intervention theory suggests the addict will either say "yes" or "no" *during* the meeting when the offer of help is made. But this is misleading since most addicts react to the offer of help with crisis.

Families often conclude, based on what they've been told, that such a reaction indicates the addict is either *not ready* for treatment or that he must *hit bottom*. Not only does the intervention end with the addict not going to treatment but, because the family did not anticipate the crisis and instead sees the intervention as a disaster or failure, it is ended prematurely when success was actually within reach. Bluntly put, this is why traditional intervention models tend to have such abysmal success rates.*

The most common scenario is for the family to *plan* the offer and then *make* the offer; then the addict will have a crisis, either during that meeting or shortly thereafter.

* *"As a generalization, we have found that about one-half of all interventions we have participated in have resulted in the person's going to some type of treatment."* ~ *Page 114, Substance Abuse, Information for School Counselors, Social Workers, Therapists, and Counselors. Second Edition, Gary Fisher; Thomas Harrison. ISBN 0-20-5-30622-5*

As long as his family has successfully kept a collective cool head, has continued selling the aesthetics of the program, NOT changed direction and has kept or put the ultimatums in place, the addict will soon realize his crises are no longer effective, at which point the family will likely see the beginnings of a negotiation.

It's a lot like hooking a big fish. Expect a fight and, when you're about to get it in the boat and you've got your net in hand, expect another one. And, when you're on your way back to shore, confident your fish is secure in the cooler, you'd better make sure that cooler is locked because he may fight you *again*.

The forms that crises take are not important if you recognize that they are mostly efforts at control.

Here is an example from one addict during the loss of his job:

"There's this one manager at work who's had it in for me. He blames me for what others are doing, and he pushed me too far so I told him off. So now they want to talk to me in the office on Monday, and I'm suspended until then."

In truth, the addict has *already* lost his job due to being tardy or absent, a direct result of his drug or alcohol abuse. Blaming others is how he begins the cycle of self-protection and abnegation of responsibility.

Here's another example. The son (who is out of money and has been kicked out of the house) calls his father and tells him the following:

"I owe these drug dealers some money, Dad, and I think my life is in danger. They stole my wallet and it has your home address in it. They said if I don't pay them $200, they're going to hurt my family!" This example is from my own playbook. What *actually* happened was that I had run out of drugs. (*Yep, I was the addict*).

I just needed more money to buy more drugs. *The goal of my entire crisis, my ruse, was to get money for drugs.*

I came up with an extreme situation I thought my dad would buy into. And, sure enough, he did. He was so pissed he almost cried. He "had had enough of my f**king problems."

The only thing that mattered to *me*, however, was to show enough remorse to be believable so I could get the money, get the drugs, and get to a quiet place and get high.

I did an intervention with a kid who was 17 years old and addicted to meth, pot, and alcohol. We did the intervention and it went smoothly, the kid was in treatment within five days. A week later, however, I got a call from his father. He was in a panic, telling me his son was back. Apparently the mother—after having worked tirelessly with me for five days to get the kid to the program—had driven to the treatment facility, picked the kid up and brought him back home!

I had a feeling I knew what had happened but I waited to hear the mother's story. Sure enough, this is what she told me: Her son had called her from the facility and told her *horror stories* about what was happening to him there. He told her about how the Health Department was visiting the facility because of the unsanitary conditions there. He told her things they were "making him do" that were morally questionable. He *demanded* to come home. He acted genuinely frightened, promising earnestly and sincerely that he would get help at a "normal" treatment center the *moment* he got home. His mom, now horrified that she had made the wrong choice, raced to the treatment center and pulled him out. She did this *despite* what the facility staff told her *and* despite what she would have found out had she taken the time to *look*.

118

She didn't want to risk that he might be telling the truth, and he took full advantage of it. If you ever run into this, go visit the treatment center and make sure your loved one is not in the same room when you're taking your tour.

The bottom line: The kid had finished detoxing, wanted out, and fabricated stories which he played on his mom. He made it into a *crisis* in order to get away from having to do the program. He controlled the situation by turning it into a crisis. *Instead of calmly investigating things, his mom panicked*.

If his mother had spent just *a little time* looking at what was *actually* happening at the center, as opposed to listening to her drug addicted son, things might have turned out better. Instead, the kid came home and was shooting dope that same day. Then he stole a bunch of guns from some Hells Angels and went on a year-long binge, *much worse than before*. True story.

Another example of crisis as a means of control is a story about a client whom I'll call Abigail. Her husband Jim, after a heartfelt outpouring of love and a plea from his family to get help, instead of humbling himself exploded into a hostile rage and told his wife, his two daughters and me that he had no intention of doing anything but sitting in the basement and smoking crack. He actually dared his own wife and kids to try to stop him.

Without going into the details which led to it, I advised Abigail to get a restraining order. The next day she went to the courthouse, told the judge her husband had threatened her, and was granted the restraining order. The next day Jim was served by the sheriff and forced to leave the family home. Within a few days, Jim had run out of money and, in order to get back into his house, he created a massive crisis with one of his daughters by calling her and painfully telling her he was homeless and hungry. He even had the gall to offer to forgive them if he could just come home (big hearted guy, right?)! The daughter, deeply moved by her father's story and believing him, convinced Abigail to have the restraining order lifted and let Jim back in the house.

No sooner was he home than he was ripping into his wife, blaming her for having the *nerve* to do the intervention, accusing her of being cruel, and (surprise) went back to doing drugs and drinking just like before. Therefore, if you hire an interventionist, follow his instructions. The price Abigail paid was that now, having violated the Restraining Order she herself had requested, she was unable to return to the judge and request a new order, so now Jim was in the house and she became the one who had to move out.

The crisis Jim presented was that if she got him off the street, he'd be able to eat and have a place to stay. The case he was trying to make was: How could she be so heartless to have made him homeless?

The *fact* was he *had* a place to stay: a treatment facility on 30 acres of southern California mountains, with tennis courts, a swimming pool, satellite TV, and great food!

So how is it he didn't have a place to stay?

This is a perfect example of the child-tantrum analogy. He was like the child who yells, "I don't wanna go, I don't *wanna* go, I don't *wanna* go." And his wife says, "Okay honey, you don't have to go to treatment if you don't *want* to. Come back home, and we'll work on things. We'll get you a good doctor, and we'll get you a therapist, and we'll get you to some AA meetings and maybe we can put all the pieces back together ourselves without all this pain and heartache," when in fact the pain and heartache is exactly what Jim created in order to get Abigail to fold up.

If Abigail had continued with what she knew to be right, not giving into his fake state of surrender, the likelihood is good that Jim would have chosen treatment. Instead, she panicked and gave in.

The addict will do anything *but* what the family knows he needs to do, which is a comprehensive, long-term program. Why? Because true rehabilitation is a hard road, and why go down a hard road when you can simply take a hit or a drink and forget all about it for one more day?

Choosing a Program

"Every battle is won before it is fought."

~ Sun Tzu

There are *enormous* differences between programs. What works for one will not necessarily work for someone else.

The right program needs to be solidly in place *before* an intervention can begin. Don't make the mistake of thinking you're going to choose a program *during* an intervention, and do *not* hire an interventionist who tells you that you can decide on which program to choose *as* you do the intervention. I'm not saying you can't you choose a program quickly, but you don't want to do it amidst the demanding environment of an active intervention.

Also, you don't want to be one of those families that flies toward whatever program promises the least resistance from the addict. That is *not* the way to choose a program. If you take the path of least resistance, you will end up on the path of least success.

Program Philosophy

When choosing a program, what matters most is its *philosophy*, and its reputation for delivering that philosophy effectively.

If you compare different philosophies side by side, one will probably ring truer than the others for the person you are trying to help.

The dominant program philosophies in the industry are the twelve-steps (Alcoholics Anonymous and Narcotics Anonymous), Cognitive Behavioral Therapy (CBT), Narconon (a holistic, residential program),

Teen Challenge (a Christian-based, retreat-style program for youth), and of course there are others. I am neither endorsing nor disparaging any program, that's not what this book is about.

Once you've picked a philosophy you believe is best suited for your addict, move on and choose a location, amenities, price point and length of stay.

For example, if you are looking at two, twelve-step programs side by side, one offering horseback riding in an expansive ranch setting with yoga and a vegan chef, while the other program offers only satellite TV, the fact is, you're really only looking at *one* program–the twelve-steps, packaged in two different ways. If you're looking at the Narconon Celebrity Center in Ojai, California and the Narconon, New Life Retreat in Denham Springs, Louisiana, you are looking at only *one* program.

Shop for a philosophy first. *Then* look for location, amenities, etc.

In ten or fifteen years it won't matter if there was a helipad or horses or if they offered vegan cuisine. Those things are not fundamental to the repair of the condition of addiction. The *only* thing that will matter is whether the person you are trying to help now is still doing well and *that* boils down to program philosophy. Keep in mind that in today's world of recovery, hybrid programs are quite popular. What you want to look at is a programs track record, and its ability to return an addicted individual to a sane and happy state.

Your main goal is a successful life for the addict, and a good program is more important than other considerations, especially the difficulty of getting the addict to go. If you think you're making life easier by choosing a program that is closer, or chosen by the addict, down the road you'll regret not having made the right choice in the first place.

Letting the Addict Choose the Program...*Really?*

Would you go out right now and find a *using* addict or alcoholic to consult with in terms of which program is the best choice to help someone you love? Of course not. *Then why ask the one sitting in front of you?* This may sound harsh, but it's true. *Don't ask your addict to choose his own program.*

The program you choose will be *the* determining factor in whether the person you are trying to help recovers his life and whether that recovery will be permanent, *so don't bring an active addiction into the decision-making process.*

Families often believe that if they involve the addict in the decision, he will feel more ownership, agree more readily, and do better once he's there. In fact, the *opposite* tends to be true. By allowing a using addict into the selection process, you're also allowing in all the neuroses that come with his condition. Believe me when I tell you that using addicts and alcoholics can sound quite sane even when a myriad of gears, agendas, and mania are at work, mechanisms that can *easily* undermine the choosing of a good program. I see it all the time. The family will be on a good path to choosing a program including a list of priorities that makes sense and a commitment to results, then they allow the addict to get involved. What was once a solid plan is now suddenly a list of questions. The goal becomes whatever is shorter or easier as opposed to what is effective. The conversation becomes controlled by the addict, not out of concern for his own treatment but because of his fear of what treatment might entail. Further, the conversation becomes focused on what he needs to do to satisfy the family as opposed to what he needs to do to regain his life.

Or, when that subject comes up, he emphatically insists he can do it on his own and all he needs to do is detox. Before you know it, you'll have agreed to a one-day, home-based program.

I am *not* suggesting you tell the person you love he is incapable of making a good decision about the program. What I *am* saying is that addicts are *de facto* incapable of it; the condition they are in makes it so, regardless of how reasonable they may appear to be or how inclined you are to believe them.

How the addict conducts his decision-making in other areas of life will give you an idea of the result you can expect if you let him choose his own program. Look at things he has attempted recently. How did they turn out? When faced with a crisis, how well does he cope? Is he honest and dependable? Does he think things through to the most logical and best solution, or does he justify traveling along the path of least resistance and then disappoint (or blame) everyone else when things don't work out? Based on *honest* answers, do you think it's a good idea to let that person choose his own program?

And if you base your choice on what you think the addict will be most *willing* to do, *you are putting the addiction in charge of the decision.* This is not only bad for your future, *you are also shortchanging the addict.* The best decision will be made by sober, objective members of your team.

Having said all of this, you can give your addict the *illusion* of choice.

Many programs have more than one location, so once you've decided on which philosophy is the best fit, you can offer to let him choose the location.

I would not, however, offer more than two choices since that might give your addict the impression he can choose any program he wants.

Intake Counselors

During your search for a treatment program, you will receive advice and guidance from a number of different sources. You'll be speaking with friends and family, you'll be looking at websites and ultimately you'll be speaking with intake counselors, also known as admissions counselors, registrars, etc.

Whatever his or her title, the person on the other end of that 800 number is going to become your main source of information about the program you're looking at, so it's important to understand a few things before you make those calls.

First, all program representatives are biased toward the program they represent. Nothing wrong with that. It is what it is.

Additionally, an intake counselor's livelihood may be determined by how many clients he gets to come to that facility. I'm not suggesting there's anything wrong with this either—it's how commerce gets done—but, since what you're going through is a highly emotional process, it's important to have your eyes open.

My advice? Don't ask the intake counselor from Treatment Center A what he thinks about Treatment Center B. That's like asking the Honda salesman what he thinks about Toyotas. Both are good cars, but you *can't* expect an objective answer from the salesman. *Keep your list of competing programs to yourself. You* need to be in control of your communication with intake counselors, not the other way around.

Every intake counselor will tell you *his* program is the be-all, end-all of treatment programs, and *maybe it is*, but that's for *you* to decide.

I'm not trying to vilify intake counselors. As an interventionist, I work with them all the time and, believe me, they are *the most* devoted, caring and patient individuals on this planet. All I'm saying is to take what they tell you, compartmentalize it from what other intake counselors are telling you and compare the information side-by-side *for yourself.*

Length of Stay

The length of the program you choose *is* important.

In addition to the initial detox process, it takes time for any addict to unload the weight of his transgressions and repair his sense of honor, integrity, ethics and conscience. Thirty-day programs are by far the most prevalent, but tend to have lower success rates when compared to longer, more comprehensive programs. Most 30-day programs have evolved, however, and are now supplemented with generous aftercare to be more effective over the long term. If a 30-day program is the only thing on the table, find out what kind of after-care your loved one will have when the residential part of the program is over.

I favor programs with a *minimum* duration of 60 days. After that, a person can be in good enough shape and have enough of a grasp of the program to pick up and carry-on for himself. This is what one looks for.

In my opinion, programs over six months in length tend to be overkill, but many recovering addicts benefit from staying in programs as interns or becoming staff as a means of achieving long-term stability.

Programs two or more years in length, which also put their clients to work, are mainly for hardcore cases. Take, for example, Delancey Street, famous for successfully rehabilitating hard-core clientele.

Families often tell me they think the longer the program, the better. I understand that viewpoint but the fact is, it's not so much how long one stays as it is what happens while the person is there.

Detox programs last days to weeks and do not represent recovery; they simply provide a brief reprieve from the worst of it. The one person who may try to convince you otherwise is the addict. He will tell you all he needs to do is clean up, get a job and life will go back to normal, and, you may want to believe him. It's certainly an easier route than having to pay for and go through a 30-, 60-, 90-day or six-month program.

The mistake with this conclusion is that it targets drugs or alcohol as the cause of all problems and insinuates that by *just* detoxing, problems corollary to drug and alcohol abuse will disappear as well. But short-term detox will *not* solve the Pandora's box of problems that addiction or alcoholism have unleashed in the person's life. Those difficulties will spring right back so, if you choose the path of detox only, don't be surprised if, in a very short time, you find yourself looking at the exact same problems and behaviors you faced before.

Location

The choice of program location is more important than many families realize. Problems are created when a family makes the location of a program more important than program content, or when a family positions an addict close to home for emotional reasons.

Ten or 15 years after your addict has graduated from the program you choose; *it won't matter where he did the program.* The *only* thing that will matter is whether the program worked. And, since all programs are not equal, you must make the quality and effectiveness of the program you choose a priority *over all other considerations,* including–and perhaps especially–geography.

Consider this: Your addict or alcoholic has a bad day at the program, His roommate steals a pair of his socks, his counselor asks him to redo an assignment he feels he did well the first time, they serve a dinner he hates and, on top of it all, he gets a phone call from his girlfriend telling him she's seeing someone else.

If the program is just a few miles from home, he's going to be out of there faster than you can say "...hang in there!"

Therefore, choosing a program that is close to home is *not* a good idea! There are exceptions of course, and not all programs close to home will be failures, but finding a quality program far from home is preferable to one close by.

During the intervention, the addict is going to be afraid to leave familiar territory. I cried when *I* went. I've driven addicts to treatment, flown in with them, and watched them cry the entire way. It's difficult enough to pack up and get on a plane if you're going away to college or moving to a new city in a new state, but the addict's fears are compounded exponentially because of his drug dependency coupled with his fear of being able to leave it. It's an uphill battle to be sure.

Keeping the addict close by is an *emotional* decision, not a logical one. The ability to have more visits from the family, for example, does not increase the person's chance for success. The fact is, most families only visit one or two times during the program anyway unless they are part of intense family therapy.

If you find yourself trying to convince yourself that the shorter program closer to home is a better choice than the longer program with a higher success rate, you need to stop and think about what results you want for the person you love going to treatment.

When the addict is resolute about doing well, it may seem like location doesn't matter, but when you get that phone call with him screaming that he needs to come home, you will be glad he's not a local bus ride or walking distance away.

The exception is when the addict is the parent of a baby or small children. Even then, however, a program that is too close can be tempting for a mother who misses her kids. You may find her showing up on your doorstep, insisting that being close to her children is more important than finishing the program.

Ultimately, you need to do what's best for your addict, and this might mean making sure she's in a program she cannot leave easily. If she doesn't finish the program because it was too easy to come back home, you have in fact done her and her children a great disservice. The difficulty of completing treatment is balanced by the fact that the addict's children have a *much* higher chance of getting their mother or father back for good once this is accomplished.

Amenities

Once you have decided on a treatment program, make a list of all the program's amenities you believe would be appealing to the person you are trying to help: is it coed, does it have good food, do they make a store run on Sundays, is there a work-out area, etc. You will want to talk about these aesthetic elements in your pitch to the addict, so make sure you know what they are as if you've been there and would want to go yourself.

Knowing the aesthetics and amenities will prevent the offer of help from feeling like a prison sentence and, if you are working with friends of the addict, *getting them excited about aesthetics will also work in your favor.* It will be a lot easier to get them to help you sell the program if they can see it as a *kind* of vacation.

On the other hand, keep the extras in perspective; don't pick a program *based* on amenities at the cost of program effectiveness. There are a lot of programs with yoga, meditation, and horseback riding and while these features can enhance a person's experience, they do not provide the long-term repair addiction requires.

References

Program graduates and their families *are* willing to share their successes. A facility should be able to provide references for you to contact.

References do <u>not</u> fall under the patient-doctor confidentiality protection law, also known as *HIPPA*. Some facilities may use this as an excuse not to provide references. This should be a red flag, so if a facility will not provide references, *move on.*

And, once the program provides you with references, *contact them.*

It astounds me how many people get a list of ten references, don't call *any* of them, and *then* express all kinds of doubts about the program.

Call the references! These are people who know what the program is really like and what new clients can expect.

To those of you who think references might be "fake," *get real.* I work with programs that can provide two hundred references because they're honest programs.

Keep in mind that you may get mixed opinions from graduates and/or families about the program you are researching. This can be a good thing. *No program is a rose garden.* It doesn't matter if they have a couple of bad reviews on Google. Recovery is a rough business. I've seen my fair share of vindictive reviews. Getting to know what people dislike about a program is as important as hearing about what they think is good, but it's important to separate level headed, objective reviews and attacks. Don't disregard a program simply because it has a couple of bad reviews. Every restaurant, house cleaning service, contractor, plumber and treatment center has a few bad reviews occasionally for whatever reason. What you want is the big picture. You may want to call several references to get a general impression of what happens at the program.

The most important thing is that while the person is at the program, real repair is occurring in his life. This is what you're looking for. This is the common denominator you want to hear people talking about.

The Best Assessment

If you can, visit the facility. The best time to visit is on a night when family members of the clients will be there as well, such as a graduation.

During the intervention, the addict *will* object (see, *Handling Objections*). Some objections will be circumstantial like he can't leave his dog or he has to go to court on such-and-such a date. But if your addict targets the program as being wrong for him, you can evaluate those objections much more easily if you have visited the facility and seen it for yourself. You can respond with real descriptions of the campus you have seen, the people you have met, and the program you observed.

The other benefit comes after the addict goes to treatment. If he *then* calls and tells you the staff is trying to get him to join a cult, that he's only being fed dry rice, that the windows in his room are nailed shut and the staff guards the doors so no one can leave (these have all been used), you'll know better. Your first-hand knowledge of the program will prevent these conversations from going any further or coming up in the first place.

You can give your addict what he needs in terms of support for the future. You can tell him you understand it's difficult being there, but he'll have to stick it out (and be sure to enjoy the volleyball court), that if he needs a care package, you'll send him one. Tell him to call again to talk. Tell him you'll visit, or stay out of his way. Tell him you'll do any or all those things but his pulling out and coming home is *not* going to be an option.

If you have not visited the facility and the addict calls with stories of horror or unbearable unhappiness, what you *can* do is *assure your loved one you'll look into it, and not panic.* Then, without your addict knowing about it, go to the facility. Visit, talk to other clients, graduates and staff. This is a big request, but it's better than reacting to a horror story, pulling the person you love out of a perfectly good program, taking you back to square one, trying to find a suitable program all over again, to say nothing of repeating a full-blown intervention.

Your goal is to recognize what's happening and to maintain your perspective rather than let the addict's crisis become *your* crisis.

Hiring a Professional

Success in an intervention is much more likely if you have the help of a professional, someone who has experience but also has no history with the addict–no minefields.

Having an objective observer provides a sounding board and neutral dumping ground for the family, as well as a safe terminal for the addict.

A seasoned professional can direct you and the rest of the family through the labyrinth of chaos and upheaval that interventions often become. That said, not all interventionists are equal; I have cleaned up more than a few messes left behind by so-called pros.

In one case, the addict would not sit anywhere near me when I initially tried to speak with him. We met at a café, and he actually sat at a different table while we talked. When I mentioned this to his mother, she told me the family had recently tried to do an intervention with someone else and then told this strange story: "The last interventionist knew *Kung Fu*," she said. I was trying to see the relevance of that when she went on to describe how her son, "had been tackled ten or twelve times during the intervention by the interventionist."

Wha-??

No wonder the kid wouldn't sit anywhere near me!

Eventually, I did manage to gain his trust and get him into the program but it was an uphill battle.

Another story involved an interventionist who eloped with the female addict. Neither of them was seen until six months later after they "broke up."

Also, look out for therapists who *claim* to be able to do interventions but who don't have the track record to back it up. Do, however, consider the *experienced* therapist who has worked in the trenches and has some real successes under his belt. Chances are he or she would be a good bet.

My recommendation is to find someone who has done a lot of interventions successfully *and* who can talk to the addict from experience.

An interventionist has a vantage point of objectivity that the family does not. An interventionist has a better chance of getting the family onto a single game plan and keeping them there. Family members have an emotional history with other family members and can get off course without even knowing it. With a professional, you have someone who's your point person, your *go-to* guy.

I cringe when I hear, "We're going to give it a try ourselves first and, if it doesn't work, we'll call you." When I hear that, I feel like I'm listening to a suicide note.

A professional can work best when he can put as many of his cards on the table as possible. If you are considering hiring someone, don't roll the dice by doing things on your own first and then, when everything is messed up, call the interventionist.

Find and hire someone *before* things go south, not after.

Your Team

*"You may have the greatest bunch of individual stars in the world,
but if they don't play together, the club won't be worth a dime."*
~ Babe Ruth

An intervention *can* be done by a single person, from organizing to strategizing to delivering the addict to treatment. If you can deliver a heartfelt offer of help and use incentives and ultimatums as a way of leveraging the person you are trying to help, you *can* succeed on your own–*if this is your only option.* In most cases, however, more than one person will be involved, so I've geared this section in that direction. For those of you who are working alone, however, this entire book and everything in it applies to *you.* Working alone is also a strong case for bringing in professional help. If you can hire a professional, it will make all the difference.

There are a couple of rules I live by when it comes to the creation of a team: While no one can do everything, everyone can do something. *Everyone* has a role to play.

Individuals with the greatest influence over the addict–either emotionally, financially, or both–should be on the team; this includes parents, grandparents, children, best friends, partners and supervisors.

Often a family will try to protect the emotional states of grandparents or children by not involving them, but in my opinion, this is a mistake. Grandparents can have profound emotional effects on an addict. You may not want to tell the addict's grandparents–e.g., your own parents or in-laws, about the situation because you're ashamed but, if you know that involving them could make a big difference, then you need to do the right thing. If the grandparents might be the dealmakers, bring them in.

Take Care of Your Team

Every member of your team needs to be aware of the importance of taking care of himself throughout the intervention process. Even the most level-headed among us can lose his cool when high stress combines with sleep or food deprivation. I see it all the time.

During times of significant stress and pressure, family members need to take the time to eat and get sufficient rest. Instead of pulling your hair out, go see a movie! A comedy. Get some space, as unorthodox as that may sound. A shot of levity in your down time can help you remain sane, and when *you're* sane, your whole team will be more effective.

Patience

Something that has been a thorn in my side during many interventions is the "let's just go get this over with" attitude. It usually happens during practice runs or rehearsals of the intervention which seem to cue the authoritarians in the family to *take the helm*, acting as if rehearsing the meeting is buffoonery. Even worse, when the intervention starts to fall apart, they pass the buck and point fingers at others. In fact, this is why a lot of interventions become disaster zones. The group caves under the pressure to rush and ends up farther from success than when they started, all to save a few impatient minutes.

The shift from planning to rushing is dangerous. Making decisions motivated by nervous energy and angst is not good strategy.

Hurrying is not a strategy. Creating an even greater sense of urgency is not a strategy.

Hurrying creates a *sense* of increased activity but in reality, robs the group of its effectiveness. So let your mantra be: Planning with patience. Patience with planning.

Children

Involving children of the addict can be beneficial, not only for the addict but for the future mental health of the child. The notion that children are *too fragile* to participate in an intervention is simply not true—*as long as* they are not placed in harm's way.

Children can be *the* determining factor in the outcome of an intervention, and I have never met a child who didn't want to help.

The most common reason families resist the idea of involving children is a desire to protect the child from any further damage than what the addict has already caused. That said, a child can touch places in the addict's heart that others simply cannot reach.

You should not be afraid to include a child in the intervention process. There are many ways to do it without endangerment or risk. In almost every case where I have included a child, the intervention has turned out well because of it.

The questions are: "how" and "when"? Having the children of the addict in the group when the offer of help is made might not be appropriate, but children who are old enough to do so can simply ask their parent to get help. You must make sure, however, the child feels secure and safe throughout the process.

Teenagers might be able to sit in when the offer of help is made, but I would never include a very young child in any meeting where there is going to be intense emotional upheaval.

Someone whom a younger child trusts could ask him some simple questions about how he feels about the condition his parent is in and whether he wants his parent to get better. The answer would then be written *verbatim* and put into a letter for one of the adults on the team to read when the offer of help is made.

It's important the words in this letter represent the child's *true voice*—not changed, re-phrased or corrected. Capturing a child's own true voice can have a profound effect on his parent.

In one example, Billy might say he wants Mommy to stop sleeping all day and to be able to come to school and have dinner together and so on. Billy's *exact words* are what is powerful.

In another case, a 12-year-old girl was living with her 37-year-old mother who was addicted to pain pills and alcohol. When I asked her if she wanted her mother to get help, she interrupted me and said, "I just want to know when she is going to go." She started to cry and asked if this meant her mother would be away for Christmas. I said it would be a trade. The girl understood. She was exceedingly brave, as children often are.

She asked me, "What do you need me to do?" I told her to tell me what she wanted to say to her mother, and I would write it down and her grandmother would read it to her mother in private. The girl quietly told me her mother had ruined Thanksgiving because she was asleep all day and had ruined Christmas the last couple of years for the same reason. She told me she wanted her mother to remember her birthday this year and to have a cake.

When the letter was read during the offer of help, there wasn't a dry eye in the house. The mother stopped fighting and went to treatment without question.

Telling a child disturbing things about his or her mother or father isn't going to help your case. Kids don't need to know all the details of what happens during an intervention. Keep your focus on getting the child to tell you what he or she believes. The insight you get back might surprise you.

Child Protective Services (CPS)

In one case, an addict was living with her baby and a known drug dealer in a *tool shed* without power or running water. Broken glass, tools and other dangerous items littered the floor. The mother had been seen smoking meth in the room *next* to the room the baby was in. When we called CPS, we were told, "We can't do anything unless she is smoking meth *in the same room as the baby."* We all just stood there, listening in stunned silence to the distant voice on the little cell phone speaker.

In my experience, CPS has never been much help in terms of what an intervention may require. Their inquiries can be long and drawn out, and the results are not always helpful. For example, they may decide the child *is* in danger and take the child into custody, but once in custody, the child may be *immediately* placed in foster care and protective orders made which may prevent the parent from seeing his child for a very long time. *Are you ready for that?*

Or, if CPS doesn't feel the child is imminent danger, the agency may decide to do nothing. This can give the addict a sense of empowerment and make the intervention more difficult.

Keep it inside the family. Get someone in the family to take custody of any children. Keep CPS and similar agencies out, unless the child *is* in imminent danger and there is nowhere else to turn. Just keep in mind that official involvement can open a Pandora's Box, so any decision should be made *conservatively* and with extreme caution.

Babies

Both mother and baby are going to be better off if they're not separated while the mother is in treatment but in doing an intervention, above all else, *do the right thing for the baby*.

Whatever needs to be done *must* be done to get the mother into treatment and the child to a safe place while the mother *fully recovers*.

This needs to be done as lovingly as possible—*but* <u>*treatment*</u> *needs to be the priority*. A new mother might try and convince her family that her love for her children is enough to overcome addiction or alcoholism all on its own, but there is plenty of evidence to the contrary. In the long run, it's better for the mothers of new babies to put their attention on their program.

If you consider delaying the intervention because you don't want to separate mother from child, think about how you will feel if you leave the baby in the care of the addict or the alcoholic and get a call one night from police telling you the child has died in a car accident when the mother was drunk or fell asleep at the wheel; or the mother goes off to make a buy, gets her dope, shoots it or smokes it, and ends up leaving the baby without any care for hours on end; or, because the mother is spending all her money on drugs or alcohol, the child is denied proper food and nutrition, supervision or education. *These are real possibilities in terms of what's on the table when it comes to the drug-addicted mother of a small child or baby.* As important as any of the foregoing, in the case of nursing mothers, is the fact that the drug and the addiction to it are passed on to the child.

There are treatment centers that specialize in helping women who are pregnant women, or who have small children. They allow long visits and all the clients share common issues and face similar struggles.

Charting a path in this situation is never easy, but it is far preferable than getting that call.

Flies in the Soup

Addicts are often the way they are, in part, because of the way they have been treated by other people. I'm not saying an adult addict is not responsible for his own condition and recovery; he is, *but* emotionally-abusive family members can adversely affect how things turn out.

People can claim to want to help but can actually sabotage efforts by pushing for things like involuntary commitment to psychiatric hospitals, cutting the person off without a solution in place, or working hard to convince everyone the addict *deserves* to be in his current condition. He'll say things like, "If he wants help, he'll have to ask for it." Or, "He made his bed; now let him sleep in it." Statements like these may sound reasonable, but the result is they justify doing nothing to help someone who really needs it.

People like this tend to be self-serving. They may not really want the person to get better, even though they'll never admit it. They become indignant at the mere suggestion they want anything other than to help, but these people invalidate efforts that might help and otherwise interfere with the success of the intervention process.

If you have someone like this in your family, you might even find that that person helped the addict get started on drugs in the first place—a parent or older sibling who influenced the addict as he was growing up, helping him get high, and then, later in life, invalidating, blaming and talking down to him by suggesting he has a chemical imbalance or needs to be put on psych meds.

Be careful whose advice you follow, regardless of how authoritative he or she may be.

If you find yourself tempted to go down a road you instinctively know is wrong simply because someone close to you is advocating it, trust your instincts and do what you think is *best* for the person you are trying to help.

People like this are not always easy to spot but, if you have one in your family, you'll know what I'm talking about.

The Confession

"Always tell the truth, even if you have to make it up."

~ Unknown

"How will you get him to admit he needs help?"

Aside from being one of the most common questions I get asked, this question first motivated me to write this book.

When I began working as an interventionist, I discovered many families believed they needed to get their addict to admit to his need for help in order for treatment to be worth the investment. This may *sound* logical but as an ex-addict, it's always been puzzling to me.

If recovery depends upon what one does or doesn't admit to his family before he goes to treatment, wouldn't recoverees cite this as a reason for their success? But, *they don't*. And, contrary to popular belief, the *reason* they don't is because recovery is *in no way* dependent upon what the addict admits to his family during an intervention. *That whole idea is a myth*.

When was the last time you heard *anyone* in you know in recovery, refer to his success as being the result of what he admitted to his family *during* his intervention? I can't think of a *single* example.

What happens in treatment, however, *does* determine success or failure: the connections an addict makes, the realizations he has, the people he meets and works with, the repairs he makes while he's there, and everything else that happens to him during his rehabilitation. What motivates us to do an intervention is the hope the person we love will come out the other side with a real chance at happiness.

During an intervention, getting your addict to admit to his need for help, or to the severity of his condition neither increases your chances of getting him into a program, nor does it predict how well he will do once he gets there.

I do understand that a first step in just about any therapy is for a person to face his problems: Facing problems *is* necessary to overcoming them—I get that—but in terms of an intervention, your role is not to play therapist. *Your* task is to be the mechanism that gets your loved one to arrive at treatment so therapy can take place.

If your loved one cuts his hand and is standing in front of you bleeding *and* is telling you it isn't as bad as you think, you're *still* going to do whatever you need to in order to get him to the hospital and *don't have to* get him to admit he cut his hand more badly than he thinks. While you're at the hospital and he's telling you he can take care of it on his own, you're going to do whatever you need to do to make sure he sees the doctor. Once he sees the doctor and realizes he really *did* need to be at the hospital—now thankful for you getting him there—you can take your loved one's hand, look him in the eye and say, *"Even though you were not able to see what I saw, I did what needed to be done."*

The Denial Myth

There is a corollary belief that if a person does not *admit* to having a problem, he does not *know* he has a problem.

Many people see this as a lack of self-awareness on the part of the addict. I can assure you, it is not. It's simpler than that.

If your loved one told you he went to the library last night when he was at a bar drinking, does that mean he *isn't aware* he was at a bar drinking? Of course not–he's *lying*.

Denial is *not* complex psychology. People talk about addicts as being "in" denial, as if it's some kind of box, but actually it's more two-dimensional: on one side is the truth, on the other is fiction.

Denial is *lying*, plain and simple, either because the person doesn't want to get caught, expose himself or is too ashamed, angry, guilt-ridden or distrustful. Admitting one is powerless over drugs or alcohol, for example, is for many a necessary first step to recovery, but *nowhere* does it say that admitting something *to one's family* is necessary, except in some literature and discussions about interventions where the idea is, in my opinion, completely misplaced.

Simply because your addict doesn't admit something *to you* does not mean he isn't miserable. Just because he tells *you* he does not want help, does *not* mean he does not want help.

In other words, if your addict is in denial when he arrives at the program, *fine*. This is part of what any quality program is designed to address. If he tells you he's willing to address his opiate addiction but plans to smoke pot for the rest of his life, *fine*. Again, this is something any program worth its salt is going to address. If he tells you that *you're* the one with the problem and the only reason he's going to the program is to make you happy, smile and tell him, *fine*. The purpose of any good treatment program is to, at some point, shift the addict from seeing himself as a victim into a condition of responsibility, not only for himself but for others. So as long as he makes it to the program where he can begin this and come back to life, make new friends and have some wins, nothing else matters. *The only thing that matters is to get your addict to arrive, and start!*

Do not look for the condition to begin to resolve itself <u>during</u> the intervention.

I once got a young man into treatment after months of his bellowing against it. All the way to the program he denied his condition was as bad as his family said it was and certainly not bad enough to justify treatment. He insisted his family was wrong and said the only reason he agreed to try was because he had nowhere else to go. Upon arrival, he called home and cursed his family, swearing never to speak to them again and predicting someday they would see just how wrong they were. Two weeks later, after going through withdrawal from several years of opiate use, he told his detox supervisor he was happy to finally be on the road to recovery and forever grateful for whatever his family did to get him there.

In the world of recovery, some of the best success stories come from very unlikely beginnings.

Big picture realizations can and will occur after your addict is in treatment, once he's off the drugs and alcohol and beginning to get control of his life again. The important thing is that the addict eventually realizes these things for *himself*, not that he confesses them to his family.

Bottom's Up

Some people say an addict or alcoholic who is in denial hasn't hit *bottom* yet, but the concept itself is problematic. First, there is no such place as "bottom." It's an abstract idea. Some see it as a kind of plateau the addict reaches, a point at which reason somehow smashes its way out of the coffin of addiction, and the addict, tucking his tail between his legs, comes begging for help. Trust me–this is a contrivance. I'm not saying that people don't give up and ask for help. They do; many reach a point where they can't take it anymore and stop. There are also a lot of people who reach a point where they can't take it anymore and *don't* stop. So, is there such a thing as *hitting bottom* for some people? Yes. Can you count on it to happen at a certain time or in a certain way with your loved one? No. This is why families who need to do an intervention should go ahead and do it.

Dealing with Denial

The easiest way to deal with denial is to let go of the notion you must get your loved one to admit he's an addict or alcoholic, any need *you* have for him to refer to himself in that way.

When an addict tells me he's *not* an addict, I don't argue; I have no need for him to tell me he's an addict. It doesn't benefit either of us, and my pressing him on the subject will probably set things back before it moves anything forward. I'm not there to evaluate him. I am *only* looking for a way to get him *to* the program.

That goal is much easier to reach if you do not make the addict wrong, invalidate him, try to wring a confession out of him or label him (even if you're certain he deserves it).

Throughout an intervention, *taking a position* is a better solution than trying to write scripts in your head. Take the position that, although you may not be the one to evaluate whether your loved one is an addict, his current choices are taking him down a road you're *not* willing to take, but you *are* willing to be part of his life and support him if he gives the program a try.

This is a strong position and does not require you to evaluate your loved one's condition *for* him, blame him or inflict treatment on him as if it's a punishment. You're opening a door to a road you *are* willing to go down and closing the door to a road you are not.

Your task is to deliver him to the front door, to be supportive of him while he's there, and to plant your feet firmly so he stays.

This may not be easy but it is simpler than many would have you believe. Keeping things simple like this will be what opens the door to a new life for the person you love.

The Offer

"Anything I've ever done that ultimately was worthwhile initially scared me to death."
~ *Betty Bender*

The first thing I do, after being introduced to the addict by someone he trusts, is to sit down with him away from the rest of the family and describe the program. I begin timidly, even apologetically. This places the addict in a position of perceived control.

I talk about my struggle with depression, with drug use, with my family and with life in general. I talk about how I'd always known I'm more than somebody stuck in a room using drugs. I talk about how, even though I knew I could get better on my own, I also knew I needed to get away from where I was living, where I was working, and be away from my family and my friends.

I make sure to include a full-color description of the program in my story, discreetly inserting remarks about the amenities, and early on I tell the addict how much his family is concerned about him and that I'm there because they want him to get help and they don't know what to do anymore. Then I thank him for listening to me, again placing him as the person in charge, and tell him that regardless of what he decides to do, at least he'll have the information about the program on the table, a show of respect toward him on my part.

So even though I'm working behind the scenes to plan every step—the use of leverage, the delivering of ultimatums—the addict has the impression I'm there at the behest of the family simply to describe the program and to answer any questions.

This also sets the stage for the future since it makes the program and me, as an advocate for it, appear to be a safe bet for the addict if and when we begin to play hardball. If he finds himself up against the ropes as the family evicts him, disconnects from him, walks out on him and so on, I need him to be able to agree to go to the program without feeling he's losing face. But *the most important thing* that I do during this first step is to paint a favorable picture of the program.

I stress the amenities: cable TV, good food, the fact that it's co-ed (if it is), a swimming pool, visiting time with people who are important to him, certain freedoms, sports or exercise, recreational activities of any kind, a nice campus location or environment and no locked doors. I avoid saying anything a using addict or alcoholic might find too heavy to deal with like going away for six months on end. Beginning the offer with a meeting between the addict and me *also* gives the addict a chance to agree to go without any embarrassing family meetings or painful ultimatums taking place.

I discreetly pull out my phone, text someone on the team to tell him I'm done with step one and, if I don't have the person's agreement as yet, let them know step two is a *go*. I then tell the addict his family all wanted to be there and tell him things but I took the liberty of telling them to write those things down, and we'll all be out of his hair in a few minutes.

As I nudge things along, I also try to keep the atmosphere *light* as opposed to treating the process like we're at someone's funeral.

The family and friends then enter and take their seats in a pre-determined order, taking care that the addict is where we want him.

I like the addict to have a little room, or to at least be sitting between relatives or friends whom he likes a lot.

Do *not* begin reading the letters by apologizing for them, asking permission to read them or with any other nervous use of time.

The Use of Letters

"A letter is a joy of earth. It is denied the gods."

~ Emily Dickinson

When I'm helping a family make an offer of help to an addict, I often rely on the use of letters. These are letters written to the addict by his loved ones which they read aloud *as* the offer of help.

The offer of help is the heart of any intervention, and letters are often the heart of how that offer is made.

Letters are a way of staying on message during the intervention. This is critical since emotions run high and can lead to disaster if unchecked.

In interventions, simplicity is king. Letters help keep the offer simple. Letters convey your offer simply and clearly. That way, when it's over your addict will know what you've said, and you'll know what you've said. In other words, by using the letters plus some opening and closing moves, you can avoid the protracted two-hour long bitch or dumping session, at the end of which, God only knows what was said! Improvised interventions turn out to be exactly that and risk devolving into a debate during which very little is communicated or remembered. Suffice it to say, letters are one of the most important tools in the intervention arsenal.

By writing down what one wants to say beforehand, one can take the time to think about what to write and how best to say it. Compare this to speaking off-the-cuff, with everyone piling in as an emotionally charged group with no roadmap and the addict blaring his disagreements in reply.

155

This is why interventions get a bad rap! Many are simply unplanned. It's like a theater company that doesn't use scripts or rehearsals. The actors *must* know when the curtain goes up, what to say, and when the curtain comes down; the theater group follows a path. Successful interventions require the same planning and execution.

If you are reading a letter, then you are saying what is written. If you become emotional or distracted, having a script right in front of you makes it easy to get yourself back on track. If the addict interrupts, you can nod your head or briefly acknowledge his comment with, "I got that. We can address that once we've said what we need to. It won't be much longer," and then go on with your letter.

Letters check emotions, mistakes, omissions, digressions, unintended remarks, attacks, etc. If you have some mess-up, don't panic. Allay your fear and then step back in as gracefully as possible. If you have planned well, every section of the meeting will have been laid out beforehand.

My format for how to compose the letters has served extremely well over the years. It keeps things on point with a consistently loving tone, allowing each person to say something truly personal without getting off track or dumping. The central meeting at which the offer of help is made should never be allowed to turn into a *dumping session* in which the addict is made to feel wrong by the group. He must be able to leave the meeting with a positive sense of the offer in his mind. If you're careful in writing your letter and you stick to it, you can accomplish exactly that–a clean offer made with a loving heart and a decisive tone.

An offer of help is the time to remind the addict of who he *truly* is. *This is the fundamental reason any family has an intervention. It is not to bring attention to bad behavior but rather to remind the addict of his real self.*

This reminder is what the addict will respond to.

There are things the addict will respond to negatively, and you'll be the bearer of those things as well, but at *other* times. Not now. This is the time to present a positive magnet for going to treatment and to emphasize the best version of the person you are helping.

At the center of an effective letter is a mirror that is held up to the addict by a loving relative or friend—not to show how horrible he is, but to see how wonderful he *can be*.

The following is the basic format I suggest:

1. Tell the person you love (care about) him and, *most* importantly, *the reasons why.*

What qualities does he have that you admire or love? What talents does he possess? List all the positive qualities the person has, even if you have to stretch it. *Tell him why you love or care about him.*

2. Tell the person what you miss about him or things you miss doing with him. Be specific. Pick something that will remind the addict of good times he's had and of the good person he's been.

Remind him he can do far better than he is doing now and he can be that better person again. Talk about what you want for the future. *Write from the heart.*

3. Tell him if he decides to go, you will be there for him when he goes, while he is away, and when he comes back. Tell him if it means staying out of his way, then you'll do that.

4. Name the amenities.

List features of the program you think he might like: co-ed, satellite TV, outings, doors that are not locked, volleyball, good food, visits, custom programs, religion (or no religion, depending on your own values), gradual and pain-free detox (especially important for addicts on heroin, oxy, methadone, pain-killers and for people trying to come off psychoactive drugs such as anti-depressants), alternative pain management, freedom to use the phone, pizza night, yoga, weight room, exercise classes, sauna, pool, lake, etc. If each person names a couple of things, by the end of the meeting a nice image will have been placed in your addict's mind.

5. Tell him that this is *his* choice.

Tell the person it's his decision whether to go to the program or not and you have made your own decision about how *you* are willing to participate. Tell him if he decides to go, you will be there for him in any and every way you can be. However, if he decides not to go, you can no longer participate in the choices he is making. You cannot finance him, house him, stand by and watch his decline or pretend things are not as bad as they are. If he chooses not to give the program a try, then you can no longer be a part of the life he is choosing to live.

6. Deliver your ultimatum if you have one.

The concept here is as vital as the message. If you have been paying the addict's rent, for example, tell him if he doesn't agree to go to the program you're no longer going to help him financially. Your message is not that you are punishing him for not going to the program but rather that you cannot participate in his decision. You can't be a part of the life he is choosing so it's a matter of your self-preservation and your integrity, not punishment of him. He has a choice whether to give this program a try, and you also have a choice. You have a decision about how you will or will not participate. That is how you present an ultimatum.

You are taking a new position. The addict needs to see a different determination in you and the letter is the place it starts.

7. End on a positive note.

Tell the person you hope he takes you up on your offer and all you are asking is that he give it a try.

In summary, the rules for letters are:

No negativity—the letter is not for you to unload

No references to the addiction except to suggest he is *lost to us*—that sort of thing

No drug references

No listing of wrongdoings

No baby stories

No push for major changes, i.e., breaking up with current boyfriend/girlfriend, moving to a new location, changing career or school—nothing major like that, unless it is an incentive.

Sell aesthetics

Sell the program *and* what the program can do for him

Never give the letter to the addict to read instead of reading it yourself.

Keep the offer based on love

Offer a lot of support if he agrees, none if he doesn't

Keep away from issues that will unnecessarily ignite the addict

Pictures can be good

Ultimatums are difficult to give but essential to the process. If you are a person who can use leverage, don't wimp out; it *must* be in your letter.

Reading the Letters

Your letters will constitute 90% of what is said during the meeting when the offer is made.

The letters *are* the offer.

Don't be shy or embarrassed. The intervention will flow *much* better if managed through letters as opposed to everyone speaking off the cuff.

It's important each family member knows in what order the letters will be read. This will eliminate awkward silences during which you're trying to organize yourselves.

Make sure everyone writes a letter, even if it's just a note. Letters are also a way of including people who are too far away to attend the meeting.

I understand some of you are going to feel awkward or feel it's less personal than conversationally telling the person how you feel or possibly letters are silly at some level. Trust me when I tell you when you're in the middle of making an offer to the addict and you're getting nervous, blanking on what you'd planned to say as the addict blurts something out at you that fills you with resentment, you'll be thankful you have your letter.

Put your heart into the letter you write. This is your chance to reach the person you know is really in there. This is your chance to remind the addict of his or her *true* identity, *why* you love him and *why* you want him back. Be specific. Keep in mind listing these qualities will be *flattering* to the person you're reading the letter to, so be expressive and caring.

Select the most objective person and make sure everyone knows his letter will be proofread by that person. This may be enough to prevent

160

people from writing anything inappropriate or something that would instigate unnecessary conflict. By the same token, whoever is doing the proofreading must not do any judging or rewriting. The communications do not belong to the person doing the proofreading; the communications belong to the people who wrote the letters. People can say whatever they want as long as it isn't scolding in its delivery, or invalidating toward the addict. A letter should never come off like a laundry list of complaints. Remember that the addict is already feeling as wrong as he can possibly feel, even though he'll be telling you you're the one who's wrong. Your purpose in reading your letter is not to make him *more* wrong. Your purpose is to give him hope, to give him a way out and to then, as much as possible, corner him into doing it using ultimatums.

The timing for the family to read the letters is right after the offer has been made by the interventionist or by a family member, and the addict has turned it down. Obviously if the addict agrees to go during that initial meeting there's no need for the letters, but the fact you're doing an intervention means that the likelihood of that happening is pretty much zip to none.

Plan the reading of letters down to the last detail. Decide who will enter the house first and where each person will sit, including the addict. Then without apology, explanation or preamble, sit down and begin reading.

Organize the reading of the letters by starting with someone the addict likes or respects a lot. Put the letter writers with less impact in the middle, and end with the person from whom the addict will most want to hear.

For example, the grandmother might start since the addict isn't likely to shut her down, then the grandfather, then the sister, then the parents and then at the end you could have the best friend.

It all depends on the relationships. It is important to start and end with people for whom the addict has the greatest affection and respect.

The first person might say something like, "There are some things we would like to tell you." But do not ask permission. Just do it. Once the first listing of all the wonderful qualities the person has starts sinking in, the addict will usually chill and listen. This is also why you always start with the person the addict is most *likely* to listen to, not someone he feels he *must* listen to This needs to be a person he respects, trusts or likes enough to sit still for.

This meeting is not an argument about *whether* he should go. It is, in fact, an offer of help and a statement from the family about that, combined with disconnections and ultimatums. None of this is a *debate*. The offer of help is a *message*.

Again, avoid condescension, meanness, anger, self-righteousness and, above all, do not invalidate the addict. One of the most important things to maintain, as you make the offer of help, is a show of respect toward your addict. You can give him an ultimatum or disconnect and *still* show him respect. This approach will *increase* the likelihood of him agreeing to go as opposed to scolding him and making him feel bad.

At the end of the meeting, *move people out*. Don't let family members linger because things will start to get weird or drawn out and you'll lose your message.

The following letters were read in real interventions. Only the names have been changed.

Sample Letters:

Dear Brenda,

I'm writing to let you know how precious you are to me, and how much I care about you and love you. The real you is such a lovely person and I miss that person. I miss seeing many of your fine qualities and abilities like your sensitivity towards others' feelings and issues they face, helping whenever you could. Your sense of fairness and generosity. Your love of music and your ability to hear a song and be able to play it. I miss hearing you play the piano. I miss your adventurous spirit, exploring new places and enjoying just walking through the woods. I miss playing games together like cards and dominos. I miss your wonderful smile. There is so much more to you than what I see today. This is not who you really are and I would love to have the real you back.

We are offering you the opportunity to get your life back and live up to your full potential and return to being that vibrant, strong, good-looking young woman you once were. It's a program in California and uses a very different approach than you have been used to. You owe it to yourself to try. What have you got to lose?

If you accept this offer, we will support you in any way we can. You can call anytime and we will visit, and most importantly, Marcus and I will be there to support you when you're finished as well.

If you are not willing to at least give it a try we will no longer be there to support you, not for anything until you go to California. So if you ever want any support from us, you'll have to go. There is nothing else on the table, no other programs, no other locations for now. I have watched you go so far downhill. I love you too much to do it anymore. I will not watch you continue to deteriorate to the point of death. Your father and I are in complete agreement that you will have to take your things and move elsewhere, immediately, either to the program or to another place. We cannot participate the way your life is right now in any way except to offer you what we think will not only help, but at a place where you will be happy to wake up and can do things at your own pace, in a comfortable environment. Other than that, we are through.

But it is my sincere hope that it won't come to your leaving to go anywhere on your own. I'm sure you could, but to what end? I hope you will be willing to go and at least get through the first part, and then see how you feel. Give it a try. There is no group therapy. The food is very good, and from what we understand, there's plenty of it. There are the repairs you need to make and the time and space to do them, away from here. Please see for yourself how different your life can be when you can enjoy living again. We'll be here waiting for you in any way we can for this. My hope right now is that you will help us all keep this as simple as possible and just say yes. Help us create the moment when you put all of this behind you.

Much love, Mom

Dear Son,

I have a picture of you in my office, which I look at every day. I am sure you noticed it and remember it very well. That photo is ingrained in my mind and exactly how I remember you at that early age in your life. You look healthy, bright with a nice smile showing confidence. You have always been very bright, curious and engaging. Our friends marveled at your intelligence and communication skills.

164

I remember one friend telling me to buy stock in that kid because he is the most brilliant he has ever seen.

I also remember what your math teacher said about you—that you were the most intelligent student he had ever taught and he had been teaching for over twenty years.

Your intelligence, wit and academic achievement continued to grow and impress until when you decided to drop out of school. It was hard for us to fathom and accept. Sure, we have been overprotective. Sure, you had many traumatic experiences and I do not mean to make light of them. We have talked about them. But everyone, I am sure, has traumatic experiences in his life. I was punished as a child and had many spankings, even though I was a good kid and did well at school.

There are so many fond memories I have with you. As a boy who stood up for his soccer teammates and fought with kids on the other team until your coach had to literally carry you to the sideline, as an elementary school student who brought the house down in laughter for his humorous presentation, as an 8-year-old who coaxed me into daily wrestling matches which he always won, as someone who led his team into the national level earning his first away trip to Tennessee after writing the most beautiful narration for the presentation. I could go on and on. The memories are vivid in my mind, so dear to my heart and so special.

This is the son who I remember with so much intelligence, who read so much and acquired the highest ethical values, with a deep sense of justice and fairness, with intellect and disarming charm, and of course all along with those special good looks. I cannot take credit for the last one!

A battle with this destructive and deadly obsession can and will be fought and won. Your control of self and future must be regained. The good, smart and caring you is inside you trying to break out. We must give him help to free him from the prison he drove himself to. He must come back with full force, and strength, to realize the great potential that few people have, to enjoy life and all it has to offer, to travel and see so many wonderful places in the world that are there to explore, to meet and engage with many wonderful people out there, to have a career, to simply have a life.

I will never forget how caring you were during the crisis with your sister recently. You thought clearly, executed, consoled us, and helped us cope during this wrenching crisis even though you were going through so much yourself that you had to cope with. Your help was so vital for us to deal and pass through the difficult times. Without your help I don't think we would have gone through it without much more damage. It showed you cared so much not only for us but also for your sister, who loves you more than anyone else in this world. She needs you now and needs you when we as parents are long gone. You cannot let her down. Nor can you let yourself either.

Your friend, Tennyson took the initiative for which you, your mom, your sister and I will forever be grateful.

I have reached the end of the line letting you fall into this abyss, of letting you continue on this path that will surely lead to death. I cannot bear to see you die slowly in front of me, with my own help. I cannot let this happen. I am taking a stand right now, drawing a line in the sand. You have to seek the help that you need to get you out of this situation. I am here to help you do that. I have been thinking about this long and hard, losing sleep and living with torment. I can no longer do that. You have an opportunity to free yourself of your demons and live again. You have so much potential, promise and life ahead of you, you have to

166

begin NOW. What do you have to lose? I cannot think of the alternative nor tolerate it. Yes, there is hope. Yes, there is a way out.

I love you dearly and therefore I must do the right thing. There is no other choice for me. This is it.

Love, DAD

Dear Adam:

I am writing this letter to let you know (I'm sure you already do know) how much I love you and want only the best for you, and want you to be happy.

There are so many things I remember about our past that I want you to remember and think about when you think about your future. Our family (including you) has gone through a lot of good times, and we have had our share of bad times, also. They all combine to make our family, and each individual person in our family, stronger and closer together.

I remember the many times, when you were misbehaving, that Grandma had to take you out of a restaurant and walk with you until you behaved.

I remember how close you were with Pip, and how much you and your sisters meant to him. He lived just to see you guys.

I remember coaching your baseball teams. You were always very good and could have been better, but I think that other priorities started to take over.

I remember the two of us going up to the Clearwater River, in upstate Idaho to go salmon fishing. We stayed in an old hotel. We had one room for both of us, and salmon soup was always on the fire in the kitchen. We each caught a 25-pound salmon. It was so hard to land the fish and you were so tired that you were ready to go home after you finally got your fish in the boat.

I remember so many beautiful things and doing so many wonderful things (hiking, climbing, horseback riding, white water rafting, rodeo). It was a trip I will remember for the rest of my life, and I hope you remember parts of it too (although you were very young).

Our lives were filled with a lot of ups and a lot of downs. You, and by extension we, are going through a big one now. But you, and we, are going to overcome it. It is a sickness that can, and will, be cured. All it takes is determination and willpower. You know you have all of our support. We will do anything and everything to help in your recovery.

The place that has been picked out for you is a beautiful place in a beautiful setting. It is in a very quiet area near the beach. You will have your cell phone and computer with you, so you can continue to work while you are in treatment. All you have to do is tell your clients that you had to go to Florida to help with a sick parent, and that you will be back soon. It is very understandable and logical.

All I want for you is to give this place a try. Please take that first step. This is something that you can't do alone, and we are all here for you. I love you very much

Dad

Dear Tom,

I'm writing to let you know how precious you are to me and how much I care about you and love you even though you know that for sure. The real you is such a wonderful person and I miss that person. I miss seeing many of your fine qualities and abilities like: your sensitivity towards others' feelings and issues they face; helping whenever you could. Your attachment to people you care for and being there for them.

I remember my one-year-old Tom standing at the corner of the road pointing with determination to the direction he wants us to go, my strong and caring Tom, who, when I had the big accident and was moaning with eye pain and nothing was done about it till you came in and took charge and got the nurse to take action and bring the eye specialist to take care of it.

When I had my knee surgery, when my dad and brother passed away, it was you taking care of me, hovering around me asking if I needed anything. And lately when we had the crises with your sister, the strong, caring Tom I know came back momentarily and kept us focused, proposed solutions and all in all helped us cope with it.

I remember when your teacher wrote on your writing assignment that he had never had a student like you in all of his career. And when your science project was a computer program while other kids did the carnation in the jar one.

I think of your adventurous spirit, exploring new places, new people and think of the strong, good looking young man you once were. I remember when you saved your money to get me a heart necklace that I still keep. I miss your wonderful smile. There is so much more to you than what I see today. This is not who you really are and I would love to have the real you back.

We are offering you the opportunity to get your life back and live up to your full potential and return to being that vibrant, strong, good looking young man you once were. It uses a very different approach.

You owe it to yourself to try. What have you got to lose?

If you accept this offer, we will support you in any way we can. You can call anytime and we will visit whenever possible.

If you are not willing to at least give it a try we will no longer be there to support you. I have watched you go so far down hill. I love you too much to do it anymore. I will not watch you continue to deteriorate to the point of death. You will have to take your things and move elsewhere.

But it is my sincere hope that it won't come to that. I hope you will be willing to go and give it a try. Please see for yourself how different your life can be when you can enjoy living again.

Much love, Dad

Gerald,

I love you more than you know. You are my only brother. Even though I wasn't around much during your high school and college years we have always talked on the phone and hung out when we could. People were always amazed at the fact that I would actually want to go hang out with my little brother. Our family vacations have always meant the most to me. Mom and dad would get so excited about having us both around. You have always been so loving and open. I miss those family times. We have always been so close. I've always been proud of how close our family has remained over the years. You know as well as I do that there aren't too many families out there like ours. Over the past few years things have changed. We've gone from partying together and being open about life to me worrying about you and you becoming distant and cold. You and I have had many a conversation about recreational use and how to not let it get out of hand. Talking with you has not gotten us anywhere and is obviously not going to get us anywhere. I went to mom and dad many years ago and it almost killed me to have to go behind your back but I was scared and worried about you. You're not the person you use to be. I know with help you can be that same person again, happy, optimistic, outgoing. Clean you will have the world at your feet. A new beginning. We know you don't intentionally hurt us and we know you would quit all of this on your own if you could but you can't and we are doing the only thing we know to do to help you. I have helped mom and dad to find a program that makes sense to me. The program in California on the beach seems like the ideal environment. It's on the beach where you can hang out or go out to dinner. There are other people there that are your age with similar backgrounds. Even though we have found the program, we know that you are the only person that can take the steps to help yourself. Please make the right choice and give the program a chance. We are here to support you in every way. It's the only way our family can be like it once was. Dad has always taught us, family is all you have in this world so, here we are as your family. I love you very much. Sabrina

Dear Winnie,

I know that there can be no doubt in your mind how much I love you. Since the very first day that I laid my eyes on you, you captured my heart.

You are one of the most intellectual young ladies that I have had the pleasure of holding very deep conversations with. I will always remember the time down the shore when you and I opted to walk home from the boardwalk (about 2 miles).

I had such a great time and it was one of those special times we had together just being ourselves.

I remember the times that you stayed at our house and all the hours of fun you and Samantha had practicing skits for shows in the garage and in the driveway.

I remember you helping Uncle Harvey catch a snake in our back yard, and the fun you had running thru the fields to dry your hair.

You are one of the most talented young ladies that I know. You have a wonderful and loving heart, and a great sense of humor and you always make me laugh. I miss you.

I want to still have those times with you. I will always love you and you will always have a very special place in my heart that is yours.

I know that you now have a decision to make. This decision is yours, but I am asking you from the bottom of my heart to please make the right decision and go to California. This is somewhere where you can truly be yourself and no one is going to tell you what to do. You can take your time and see who you really are. I will always be here for you, Sweetheart, and I will never let go!!

Love you, Aunt J.

When the last person is done, ask the addict if he's willing to give the program a shot. Decide who will do this beforehand.

Wait for his answer.

At this point, one of three things will happen: He will agree to go, he will tell you he needs to think about it, or he'll say he won't go and start listing the reasons why.

172

If he agrees to go, the rest is *fairly* academic, although there are still some important points. For example, don't *keep* persuading him. He's bought the farm, no need to sell the chickens. Do not keep talking about the program while you help him with his laundry or tie up loose ends.

Let the addict lead conversations about treatment. I'm not saying not to bring it up at all; just don't *keep* bringing it up. You may feel relief, but the addict is feeling fear, trepidation, and possibly anger toward you and everyone else.

You should expect an outburst or two, so brace yourself and *don't* get into a fight about *anything* if at all possible. The addict may try to push your buttons, looking for any fight as an excuse not to go. If this happens, keep in mind the person in front of you just agreed to something he would rather not do. He doesn't want to feel he is being *forced* to do it, and he might feel he has very little left except his pride which, in the past few hours, has left the building. Now he is searching for control, and for you it may be like he's standing in a canoe, tilting it from side to side. Your task is to stay seated and make sure the canoe keeps moving along, as precarious or difficult as that may be.

Addicts who agree to go to treatment quickly can destabilize just as quickly.

Do not make the mistake of letting the addict sell you on the idea of going "in two weeks." *It won't happen.*

Above all else, don't get on a roller coaster. You either have agreement or you don't. It's not bobbing and weaving. Sure, allow for some back and forth–it would be a little cruel not to–but don't let the back and forth be a way for the addict to dig in and pretend the intervention didn't just happen.

If the addict flips 180 degrees, then you simply pack him up and ship him *out*, or do whatever you told the addict you were going to do if he didn't go into the program. Flip-flopping can be an effort to frustrate the family.

Handling Objections

"Don't find fault. Find a remedy."

~ Henry Ford

One of the most common questions families ask me is, *"What if the addict says 'no'?"* It's a good question since addicts saying *no* is the reason I do what I do. Interventions are the alchemy of turning an addict's *no* to a *yes*.

Handling objections is *key* to any intervention's success.

In a very real way, however, you *need* those objections. And, I'll wager you already know what 90% of them will be.

One of the first steps in any intervention is sit down with the addict, describe the program and then offer him the program using whatever means you think will work. Some of the tactics I use are described in this book. The addict, however, is not going to roll over and agree to go to treatment simply because you have solutions for his objections (maybe but unlikely). But by being prepared, you will be in a much stronger bargaining position than a family that, in the middle of a meeting with the addict, is stumbling for answers to objections they *knew* they were going to face but decided it was too much trouble or too awkward to plan for. Don't make that mistake.

Some objections are more reasonable than others. Some are obvious, even plausible, and you should have the solution to them *before* the addict brings them up.

For example, if the addict has a dog who has been his long-time and close companion, figure out who is going to take care of it while he's away. Will the dog be able to visit his owner in treatment? Is he on a special diet or medications? Line up the *who's and what's* about pet care *ahead* of making your offer.

What about the addict's apartment and belongings? Maybe the family can continue to rent his place while he's in treatment. Or, have a moving truck and a storage unit ready to go before the intervention takes place. This is a valid concern. Have a solution in place.

What if the addict is in a relationship and insists he can't leave his sweetheart? When I run into this situation, I try to get the family to get cooperation from her, even if the family doesn't like her or blames her (or him). An intervention is not the time to hash out differences between family members and a love interest of the addict; it is *only* a time to get your loved one into a program. So regardless of what people's opinions may be, I have the family offer to support the relationship during treatment by helping with visits or communication between the two. By doing this, you begin to close that door as a way out for the addict. The relationship itself can be dealt with later once the addict is in treatment so, if you need to, bite your lip while working with the boyfriend or girlfriend of the person you're trying to help. You're also placing the girlfriend into a heroine's role for supporting treatment. Stress to her that, by his going to treatment, she will benefit as well. He'll get his health back. She'll be able to trust him again. He'll be a boyfriend she can be proud of, and so on. Of course, this isn't going to work in every scenario, and it takes courage to do. It means getting into conversations you may not have at the top of your to-do list, but being uncomfortable is often part of a winning equation.

There are objections as psychological warfare which are more difficult to anticipate but which can still sink your intervention.

There's the famous *what-about-you* objection where the addict turns the offer of help around and points a finger at other family members, calling them out on their own shortcomings, habits or addictions and hoping to invalidate the intervention as a hypocrisy.

The solution for this depends on the severity of the shortcoming in question. For example, if the addict accuses a family member or friend of smoking pot occasionally, a simple acknowledgment and a promise to stop could be expressed, especially if it's a parent. On the other hand, if an addict accuses his mother of an addiction to Xanax and painkillers, and he's *right*, you've got an entirely different situation on your hands. If someone conducting the intervention is outed by the addict, you'll not only have a hell of a mess on your hands but that clear message you were hoping to deliver will be lost. If a parent or sibling has a significant drug addiction, and the person you're trying to help is likely to use that fact against you, believe me when I tell you, it's *much* better to be in front of it than for it to come up unexpectedly in the middle of a family meeting.

During the planning stages, once you identify an issue that is likely to come up during the intervention, the best way to address it is to include it in your letter, acknowledge the problem and offer to do something about it. This doesn't eliminate the subject from coming up, but it lessens the degree to which it can adversely affect the outcome and is far better than an unexpected bombshell.

Then, there is the *I-can't-go-because-I-have-things-to-do* objection.

The addict has been using drugs or alcohol for years, but when the subject of treatment is brought up, he suddenly has a schedule or a job interview! I've seen it dozens of times. In the middle of the intervention, we're making the offer of help and you can practically see the wheels whizzing around and around in the guy's head. Suddenly he announces he has a job interview the next day or the next week and can't go to treatment because he's about to achieve what everybody wants, which is for him to get back to work and be a responsible human being again.

The real zinger is how well this works! I've watched families fold up like yesterday's newspaper. The addict is sitting there with sunken eyes in a drug induced trance, not having slept for days and, with one or two statements, has his mother perched on the edge of her seat wanting to hear all about this job interview he suddenly has and thinking maybe we don't have to do any of this after all! That is a one-way ticket to regretsville.

The solution lies in your realizing that this appointment is just another effort to gain control, and *not* giving in to it. This is the addiction fighting for survival. The job interview is your opponent's move. It wants to keep surviving by creating distractions and trying to make deals. So, what do you do? You stay on course! You work as a team *and don't make deals.*

Do not allow the addict to turn the intervention into an argument about work. Working or school attendance is simply not the issue. The person in front of you, pleading for another chance if he can just make this job interview, is the captive of drugs or alcohol. You already know that. You also know he could only hold a job for a day or two and, if you want him to have a permanent job or a career, he needs to go to the program and take care of how he operates *first.*

Then there's the *if-you'd-approached-me-differently-I-might-have-gone-but-now-you've-betrayed-my-trust* objection where the addict, in colorful irony, makes the *intervention* the reason he's not going to the program. Your solution to this is to acknowledge the fact this conversation was never going to be easy and to take a strong position, but *don't* condescend. This is important. Be very matter-of-fact. Say, "Yes, it's an intervention. Yes, we did some planning without you and, yes, we're approaching you all at once because honestly we didn't know what else to do."

Make the intervention about *you*. Tell the addict you're doing this for your own well-being, your sanity and your self-preservation. You're making the offer of help willingly, but what he does is his decision. By the same token, participating in his life is your decision and right now you're not willing to do *anything* else except what you have put on the table, which is the program. This is not about asking the addict to go, and hoping that he will. Tell the person that. Be nice, but be clear. It's about your own need to disconnect from the choices he's making in his life.

You need it out of *your* life. The idea of self-preservation is a difficult one to argue with. Despite this, you should plan to hear a vigorous rebuttal. Addicts and alcoholics generally view themselves as victims of circumstance, so expect a reaction, even if you say everything perfectly. Remember it's not what's coming at you from the addict's mouth that is important; it's what goes into his ears that matters. He may be hostile, so be ready for that. Allow him to blow up but *you* stay with self-preservation, i.e., "This is not just about you (the addict). It's about my needing to disconnect from what you are doing."

Then there is the *you-guys-are-making-a-way-bigger-deal-out-of-this-than-it-needs-to-be* objection in which the addict minimizes his problem while scoffing at residential treatment as overkill. This objection is usually followed by claims about the minimal amount, if any, of drinking or drug use. The last thing you want to do is to back yourself into a corner by arguing about what is or isn't being used. That's a losing argument.

The best example I can give you is from my own conversations with addicts and alcoholics prior to making the offer. Without my even bringing it up he will say, "I don't have that big a problem. My family is making it out to be much more than it is," and so on.

My response is, "I'm not here to judge you or determine whether you even *have* a problem. I am simply here as a messenger and to assist in the process if you decide to go."

As a parent, for example, you can say it's not up to you to determine whether the person is an addict, but you are qualified to decide whether you want the person's unacceptable behavior in your life anymore (self-preservation).

You can answer by suggesting the person go to the treatment center and, if he's not an addict, they'll determine that there. Of course, you're not agreeing he could come back home after that. You're just suggesting he agree to a two-week probationary period. One way or another, you're no longer going to be involved, regardless of what he may think of his own condition.

Some objections come as threats like *if-you-make-me-go-I'll-kill-myself/ burn-the-house-down/ leave/ never-speak-to-you-again.*

The most difficult in this kind of objection is the threat of suicide. Addicts usually direct this kind of threat to the mother or, in some cases, the father. I made threats of suicide toward my mother at different times. They weren't direct threats. They were more veiled and always for the same reason: to stop her from moving forward with, say, an intervention, or whatever she was trying to get me to do.

Consider this, though: A person seriously contemplating suicide is probably not going to announce it to the world. That person is in conflict and looking for answers. What you want to do is remind him of the offer on the table.

Would this person rather kill himself than go to a treatment program—especially one that has a swimming pool, good food, comfortable beds, and so on? This is what worked with me; you can bet, I wasn't actually going to kill myself when I had such an attractive option.

Real tragedy can and does occur when the family disconnects from an addict *without* offering a solution. The most important part of your reply to these kinds of threats is to continue to paint the program as an island in the sun. For example, you might say, "I hope you don't kill yourself—I do—but that's not my decision to make. My decision is to offer you a possible way out of your current situation. There are no guarantees, but it might be exactly what you've been wanting—or at least what you need. It's a beautiful campus where you can get your health back both mentally and physically with people who care, many of whom have been down the same road you're on now. All I'm asking you to do is give it a try. We can go shopping first and get a nice steak dinner. Then I'll drive you in. Give it a try for a couple of weeks and, if you would still rather die, that's your choice to make. There are no locked doors at the program. You can walk out anytime."

The key to counterbalancing threats of violence or suicide is not to give in to the person's demands but to make sure he knows he is loved, and why he is loved and knows there's an open door to a potential solution described as enticingly as possible.

Most objections on the part of the addict are attempts to get the family to agree to a program with less commitment, a lower price tag, a shorter length of stay, etc. I consider this to be one of the most dangerous points in the intervention because I see so many parents and relatives fall prey to the promise of something easier. I call it the bait-and-switch.

The bait is that the addict finally agrees. Yes, he has a problem and things need to change. The family thinks, *"Johnny acknowledges he has a problem and needs help, that's huge, right?"* But now they're the ones on the hook and, at this point, will often make the mistake of softening up as the addict lays out his counter-offer, *the switch.*

One common device addicts use is to offer to trade the treatment program for a contract. This usually consists of a promise (on a stack of Bibles?) to stop using drugs or drinking, getting a job or going back to school and, if these conditions are not met, he will go to treatment without a fight. And to make it a real contract, the addict offers to put it all in writing.

The problem, of course, is that it *never* plays out the way it's promised. The reason is very simple: *A contract does not address the underlying condition or the reasons the addict is abusing drugs or alcohol in the first place.*

A contract will not fix the person's condition. Not one bit.

Most addicts are good at manipulating their families and especially their parents. They will look at you with tears welling in their eyes, promising earnestly and sincerely this time will be different because the intervention has made them realize things do need to change. They say they hadn't realized how bad things had gotten, and first thing in the morning they're going to get that résumé together, hit the street, get a job and again get traction in their lives.

If the family pushes back the addict will become indignant, accusing his family of not trusting him, which, in his mind, is the real problem. He thinks all he needs is for the family to believe in him and just give him a chance.

My main piece of advice here? *Don't give in.*

Even though the addict is sincere about these promises and intends to follow through, if he were in a condition to go out, get a job and start living life responsibly, *he already would have.*

Promising to stop using or drinking and get a job is not a solution. It is the promise of a solution. The heart wants to believe it, but it won't happen by virtue of a simple paper contract.

If the addict insists a contract is the simplest solution, be careful how you disagree. You want to validate the addict and his sincerity, but you *cannot* go along with his contract offer. This is easier said than done, but it's not impossible.

This basic premise applies to most objections: Whether the addict is accusing you of something, making you and the family wrong for doing the intervention in the first place, threatening to make you suffer if he's made to go to treatment or whatever, the best solution is the simplest one. Don't invalidate the addict or make him wrong or try to beat him into submission. Simply leave the original offer as the only offer.

Ultimatums; Why and How

"Courage is being afraid but going on anyhow."

~ Dan Rather

When most people think of an intervention they think of delivering ultimatums. This is why when most people think of interventions they cringe.

What they do *not* understand, is that, although an ultimatum *is* a show of force, it does not have to be delivered aggressively or condescendingly. This is key and should actually be a source of relief. An ultimatum delivered as a matter of self-preservation can be a very effective strategy in an intervention. Not only do you not have to be condescending; it's *better* if you aren't.

When my mother gave me an ultimatum to get me to go to treatment, she didn't present it as *punishment*. She presented it as a way of disconnecting *herself* from what I was doing, leaving me with the bad choices I was making. If I chose to go to the treatment program, she would remain in my life. She wasn't disconnecting from *me*; she was disconnecting from *my behavior and the destruction I was leaving in my wake*. She told me she loved me too much to watch me kill myself or to participate in any way in my self-destruction. She did not talk down to me or treat me like a five-year-old when she gave me the ultimatum. She said very matter-of-factly that if I wasn't willing to at least *try* the treatment program, she could no longer support the choices I was making and I would have to deal with the consequences of those choices on my own, without her support or the support of my family.

With the rest of the family echoing her, I began to realize it was over.

I could choose to continue with what I was doing at the time, using drugs and drinking, but I would no longer receive monetary handouts, the bits of rent paid here and there, or even communicate with my family beyond a quick hello and goodbye. On the other hand, I could choose to give the treatment program a try. My family had already described it to me in colorful detail, emphasizing the amenities like the swimming pool, a weight-lifting area, and no group therapy (something which I found appealing). If I chose the latter, I would have the full support of my mother and the rest of my family. After two weeks of *giving the program a try,* I decided to stay for the duration.

If I were to go back and identify the point at which I decided to go to treatment, it was the moment the choices became real to me.

But no one likes being the bad guy. Ultimatums are tough to deliver, but deliver them you must.

A father who has always been there and has forever said "yes" to his little princess can find himself tasked with the impossible when it comes to giving his daughter an ultimatum, being the bad guy, and saying "no" to something she is begging for. I have seen many fathers turn tail and run from this challenge. I have seen intervention blackouts when a father who was on course a moment earlier turned and refused to be—or what he perceived to be—the bad guy toward his little girl. The other side of this coin is that Daddy's little princess knows exactly how to plead a nuanced suffering that will tug on her father's heartstrings to get the financial support she needs to continue killing herself. It is one of the many horrible ironies of addiction.

One of the most difficult tasks I have as an interventionist is to convince parents that an intervention ultimatum and actual disconnection are two entirely different things.

186

Disconnection is simply that–a disconnection. It is unclipping the line and leaving nothing for the person to grab onto. But an intervention not only gives the addict something to grab onto, it gives him the Water of Life by forcing him to let go of the bottle of poison.

An ultimatum may be the most loving thing you can possibly do for the addict you love.

There are three basic types of ultimatums: *financial, circumstantial and emotional.*

A *financial* ultimatum is straightforward: If the addict is dependent on financial support from someone, the ultimatum is that the money will stop if he does not go to treatment.

A *circumstantial* ultimatum, as the term implies, pertains to things such as housing, use of a vehicle, a job, something to do with school, access to medication or something else that is meaningful or necessary to your addict.

An *emotional* ultimatum is more nuanced. For example, a grandmother or grandfather the addict is close to or respects a great deal tells the addict how much he is loved and cared about and how much the family is hoping he will at least give treatment a try. If he doesn't, that person tells the addict very plainly he can no longer support the kind of choices the addict is making and is going to cut off communication with him until he is at least willing to give the program a shot. So although it's not cutting off funding or serving an eviction, never underestimate the power of an emotional ultimatum. If I were to have to guess which kind of ultimatum has worked in most of my interventions I would have to say the emotional type. Financial ultimatums can be a big kick in the pants.

Generally, there are two ways to deliver an ultimatum. One way is to do it in anger, talking down to the person as if he deserves it because of his bad behavior. The other way is to deliver it from a position of self-preservation, lovingly and respectfully but with assurance and certitude.

The same ultimatum can be delivered with the same force and resolve by saying you can't participate in their slow suicide anymore. And then make the ultimatum real to the addict *by following through with it.*

Say for example you tell your addict very matter-of-factly you're done and your participation in his current choices is over. The next step, if the addict does not go into treatment, is to make your ultimatum *come true.*

This is the crux of many interventions when you actually follow through with the things you've threatened to do, and the addict sees it for himself.

When you deliver the ultimatum, it's likely your addict won't believe you will carry it out. So it's up to you to show him. Your addict must now see a mother or father, a sister or brother, son or daughter he has never seen before. If you have been the *soft spot* in the family, he must clearly see that is no longer the case. *This alone can turn the tables in your favor.* Again, this doesn't mean you need to be mean or be a jerk. It does mean that you need to follow through with what you've said. If, for example, he wants to play hardball about staying where he's living and you have some control over it, leave him with the loving offer of help and then arrange to get a restraining order to have him removed from the house.

This is the point where your ultimatum becomes real to him.

Negotiating and Closing

"When the result is expected to be a compromise,
it is often prudent to start from an extreme position."
~ John Maynard Keynes

Once you've done your best to offer solutions to the addict's objections, your closers come into play. These are people whom your addict loves, whom he respects, or who control his finances or circumstances.

When your addict begins to negotiate, it means he has started preparing mentally to enter the program. You can get the negotiation going with a question like, "What would it take to get you to go?" or, a close friend can say during a private conversation, "All your family is trying to do is to get you to try. If you're willing, just go and see if it's the right place for you. I'm sure you could ask for something in return." This is not so much allowing the addict to dictate terms as it is giving him a sense of control by putting him in a position to ask for something, but ultimately they are things you're already prepared to agree with.

This kind of dialogue gives the addict the sense of having some control. The family is not asking him to go away for months and months; it's simply asking him to try. I've gotten many addicts into treatment by the simple request to *give it a try*.

Negotiation is deal-making. You want to give the appearance you are making concessions when, in fact, you're pushing an agenda. You want your addict to go into the treatment program as soon as possible.

The High to Low Close

In real estate, the high close is the asking price. That's the amount the seller is asking for but, in fact, he's willing to take a lower amount. The same rule applies to interventions. Your closers and negotiators are going to try to get the addict to agree to go to the program that same day. It's not very likely the addict will agree, and that's okay. You don't expect him to agree to that. What you do then is create a scenario in which the addict will argue to go the next day, which is what you want in the first place. The addict will think he's getting *his* way but will actually be going when you want him to go. The high close is one way of accomplishing this, but you must keep a couple of things in mind.

First, you don't want to drop to a low close too soon. You don't want to ask him to go right then and there and then immediately agree for him to go later. The better tactic is to go back and forth with the addict for a little while. This will raise his determination to argue for a later time. If you continue to argue with him to go immediately, then he may shorten the time he wants to delay all on his own. This is an ideal outcome and one I've reached many times with this strategy. Don't be afraid of it. Go ahead and create an argument you know isn't real. It takes a little bit of acting skill. You need to be convincing. The addict needs to *believe* you expect him to go into the program immediately, as in, *right at that moment.* The idea is that the addict will push back and actually close the deal to go at the time you wanted him to go in the first place.

Negotiation also means listening to what the addict wants to take with him, like his phone or computer.

Typically the answer is, "Yes, of course, he can *take* anything he wants." Whether he will be able to keep it once he arrives may be a different story. You may have to bend the truth a little bit to give the appearance of accommodating these things.

180's and The Last Hurrah

"May the holes in your net be no larger than the fish in it."

~ Irish blessing

It's not uncommon for an addict to agree to go to treatment and, within the 24- to 72-hour window in which he is supposed to leave, change his mind, pull a 180 and refuse to go.

This is textbook behavior. An addict waits until everybody's worn out and then flips everything upside down and announces there's no way in Hell he's going.

What you can do is this: If you've given the person an ultimatum to either go to treatment or leave, then tell him he can leave. If you haven't given him your ultimatum, *this is the time to do it.*

This is the only time I would suggest you fight fire with fire; it's reasonable to be angry when a 180 happens. The addict is manipulating you because he's afraid of what's to come. He's like the child who is jumping up and down screaming because he doesn't want to go to the first day of school. He is doing so not because he's evil or malicious but because he is afraid.

So if you can, resist the inclination to lash back at the addict. Try to handle the situation matter-of-factly. Try to understand what's going on with him. I would caution you against expecting the addict to breakdown in tears and lean his head on your shoulder. That's just not going to happen. It's hard, but you must at least try to express understanding as you carry out your ultimatum of kicking him out, or cutting off finances, or handing him divorce papers, or taking car keys.

The most important thing to remember about the about-face, 180-degree turn, is that it is *not* uncommon. If it happens, stay firm in your position of being unwilling to participate in anything except to get him into treatment.

Blowout Before You Dry Out

One of the most common occurrences, and one of the most disturbing for most family members, is the fact almost every addict wants to have one last blowout before he dries out. The first instinct for most families is to try to police the addict and make sure he doesn't misbehave on the way into the program by using drugs or alcohol. It depends on the individual and the situation, of course, but I *do not* try to control what the addict does or doesn't do on the way to treatment, as long as he gets there. As I said, *one last blowout* is very common, and, as an ex-addict, I understand wanting a *last hurrah*. I don't encourage it, even though, in many cases, I have allowed it. When I have, it was because it helped make the entrance into treatment go without further incident. I cannot, however, legally recommend this strategy. I'm simply sharing what has worked for me at times. What you do is going to be up to you.

You need to pick your battles. My only battle is getting the addict through the front doors of the facility. When I was in treatment in 2001, a Baptist evangelist from Florida came to the program. We found out his mother had driven him and allowed him to smoke crack in the back seat the entire way since that's the only way he was going to go. He arrived extremely high but just fine and did well in the program.

Transports and Arrival

"I discovered the only way to catch a train is to miss the one before."

~ G.K. Chesterton

Your loved one has agreed to go to the program. Your task now is to get him there.

The first thing you must do is answer some sensitive questions about his transport and arrival: Who, if anyone, will go with him? How will he travel? Does he have or does he need ID? Will he try to use drugs or drink on the way? If so, what do we do about that?

On the question of who will travel with the addict, consider the whole spectrum. If the person wants to go in on his own and that actually happens, the addict who has arranged for his own flight and has made the journey on his own will have a *tangibly* higher level of ownership for his decision to be at the program, and may arrive in a *better* frame of mind than somebody who was babysat the entire time. It is something to consider. Allowing an addict to travel unescorted is fine, but it can be risky and should only be done if he hasn't broken other promises he has made in terms of committing to go.

In most cases, someone will need to escort the addict to the door. The list of candidates should begin with the person he is closest to *and* with whom he has the least risk of emotional conflict. The intense emotions between parents and addict, for example, mean there is a high risk of manipulation. The bottom line is to make the trip easiest for the person going to the program. That is your priority. And remember the staff at the treatment center can help arrange transport and should be quite adept at it.

If you're making flight arrangements; *buy refundable tickets*. Don't buy discounted tickets that can only be changed by paying a hefty fee. Regardless of promises made or the degree of sincerity behind them, the chances of a using addict or alcoholic following his schedule or making his very first flight on time is actually fairly low, so low in fact that every time *I* make travel arrangements, I often have a back-up set working as well. Purchase a *refundable* ticket *and* you may want to make a second reservation in the same name on the next flight. Airlines allow this, and this can cover you if the addict misses the first flight which, believe me, happens *a lot.* I've had people miss up to five or six flights *in a row,* so you need to prepare for it. It's very frustrating, to say the least, while it's happening, but eventually, if you can maintain some degree of calm, he'll get on the plane. The treatment program will have somebody who can meet the addict at the airport, so transport to the program should be straightforward.

It's important for the family to stay cool if delays happen and trains and planes are missed. Don't let things build up to a big explosion. It's not easy, but that's how you succeed.

The escort should not talk about treatment or addiction while traveling unless the addict wants to talk about it. In other words, don't keep trying to convince the person that what they're doing is the right thing. They're doing it and that's all that counts at this point. Gilding the lily can only be annoying for the person you're trying to help. I'm not saying not to comfort the person or go over details, I'm simply advising for whomever does the escorting to be self-aware and not to fuel resistance by being enthusiastic yourself. Be sensitive to what your addict *is* feeling, not what you think he *should* be feeling.

194

There can be some odd twists during the transport portion of an intervention. I had a guy in Las Vegas who was so tweaked on meth he was never going to make it past TSA. My job was to get him to the program which was in Newport Beach, California, about a five-hour drive. His mother rented a big SUV for us, and he got some of his drug of choice before the trip. This was part of the deal he and I made; I drove and he tweaked out in the back seat but at the end of the day, I delivered him to the detox in one piece. He was scared but did walk through the front door and started the program.

I tell you this to show that transports aren't always easy or simple. The watchword is: Do what's going to be easiest for the person going into the program.

Even if the law does not require minors to be accompanied on airplanes, I always recommend escorting a minor every step of the way. There are so many emotional complexities for young people going into a treatment program, especially for the first time, and it's not a good idea to have them travel alone.

What do you do if your addict does not have identification? Let me tell you about two young men I was escorting to treatment, neither of whom had ID. In the first case, a senior TSA official at the airport called his Washington office which had the authority to allow my guy to travel without ID. He answered their few questions about his identity and past residences, and we were cleared for flying without any problem. In the second case, the senior TSA officials made the same offer, but my guy decided to lie and tell the man he had no idea where he used to live. He said he couldn't remember what his Social Security number was, had no idea what his mother's maiden name was, etc., so he was not allowed on the flight. It became obvious this was exactly what he wanted. Then he called his father and said that he couldn't travel without ID, which was, of course, a lie.

The bottom line is you *can* fly without identification. If you have anything with the person's name on it—an old library card, a student identification, even a prescription pill bottle with the person's name printed on the label. TSA generally accepts any and all of those as identification and, if none of these things is available, TSA can always call its Washington office from the airport in order to confirm a person's identity over the phone.

Arrival

Even after the addict arrives at the program, you can't necessarily say the intervention is over. I've witnessed a few things I think you may find very informative.

First, addicts who are new in treatment often communicate *very* differently with their parents or close loved ones than they do with anyone else. I have heard new arrivals on the phone ranting, crying, and often screaming at parents, boyfriends or girlfriends, telling them how miserable it all is, how wrong the program is, and how they don't need to be there and *just need another chance*. Then as soon as they hang up, they're perfectly fine; they go on eating, playing cards, watching TV, doing the program work or whatever. Ninety-nine percent of the time when an addict wants to leave the treatment facility, he is going to create a melodramatic, explosive crisis.

It's not a good idea for the family to be in communication with the addict during the first 10 days or so. He needs time to settle into the program. If you want to find out how your addict is doing, call the intake counselor or detox supervisor.

This way, you'll hear a little about how unhappy your person is but it won't be a full-blown knock-down-drag-out yelling match on the phone.

If you do end up in a conversation where the person is unloading on you and says he will never speak to you again unless you come get him right then and there, the key is – *Do not go and get him*! It seems simple enough but I've witnessed more than a couple of panic driven "rescues" which were nothing more than a massive manipulation by the addicts.

I can't tell you how many times I have worked with a family diligently over days to get their loved one into treatment, only to have them zoom back to the center to *rescue* their addict because they've bought into his complaints and whining over the phone!!

So what do you do if your loved one tells you about how badly he's being treated and then offers up some gory details of clients' heads being shaved or being fed dry rice or his bedroom windows have been nailed shut and guards posted outside the door? (By the way, I have not made these stories up.)

Your first line of defense is realizing *drama* is part of the picture during the first weeks of treatment, so you are not surprised. Perhaps you have also visited the program yourself and talked with the staff members, so you have your own knowledge about what goes on. If you know enough about the facility, you can remain calm and steadfast in your decision, despite your addict's railing against it. Have faith the counselors and staff are doing their best to help the person you love so he can begin the tasks necessary for his repair. The best way to keep the *drama* down is to have done your homework about the program beforehand so that when the addict brings its credibility into question, you'll know the truth. Minimizing the communication you have with your addict until he has settled in is strongly advised.

If, on the other hand, you do end up with questions about the program based on the complaints your loved one is making, the solution is *not* to pull him out of the program., Instead, go to the program yourself, or assign someone else to do it. Obviously, if the validity of the program can so easily be questioned, then you've never visited it.

If you do visit early on for investigative purposes, you do *not* want to tell your loved one about it or he will see you as an escape route. If your visit is successful, however, it will put the question of the program to rest. I strongly recommend attending treatment facility graduations if you can do so *before* the person goes in.

Until your addict is fully into the program, his visitors should be limited to the people who are not going to give into his demands or drama. If his parents are pushovers and likely to buy into his complaints, then someone else from your team should go and visit early in the program—and not alone. Choose two people who can balance each other in terms of "push-overness."

Obviously visiting the program is not always feasible, but do it if you can. If the addict complains the program is horrible and his environment unbearable, get a few references from the intake counselor and call them. Find out what people's real experiences were at the program. Do whatever you need to do to feel that you have some certainty about what's happening at the program, because 99% of the time when an addict calls his parents or his spouse or his girlfriend or boyfriend in a crisis, he is simply trying either to get high or get out of doing the program.

Try not to be cynical or insensitive. In fact, you want to be as sensitive as possible to the fact that, if it were you and you found yourself surrounded by a bunch of people you didn't know, without any of the things that make you comfortable, plus you haven't slept for days and are craving your drug of choice or a drink, you'd be bitchy too!

Every detail in every story in this book is true.
Only identities and locations have been changed.

Part IV

My *Exploding* Workshop

(Six Case Studies)

Lisa

"Medicine is the only profession that labors incessantly
to destroy the reason for its own existence."
~ *James Bryce*

I'm happily contemplating the prospect of my first Christmas with my family in several years when my phone erupts to signal an intervention.

The call is from a woman named Karen. She's looking for treatment for her sister, Lisa who is 37 and living in a converted garage in Bakersfield, a sprawling outpost in California's Central Valley.

According to Karen, Lisa is addicted to prescription drugs, taking four or five different anti-depressants and mood elevators, five powerful pain medications including OxyContin and Vicodin as well as medications for diabetes and rheumatoid arthritis, washing all of this down with liberal doses of hard liquor (I am continually amazed by the resilience of the human body.)

Essentially, Lisa is on lethal doses of contradictory medications, any one of which is highly addictive, but taken together amount to a daily game of Russian Roulette.

After Karen sketches out the situation, her mother Lori gets on the phone. There is a distinct aspect to someone on prescription drugs. From her slow, careful speech and her heavy, tired breathing I suspect Lori is probably hitting the meds pretty hard too. I mention this to Karen. She excuses it by saying her mother has Parkinson's disease, then closes off further discussion by stating she has to fight one battle at a time. This is to be her sister Lisa's intervention, not her mom's. I agree. In this case, there isn't enough money set aside to send them both to treatment. Besides, the family just isn't ready.

Sometimes a family will have more than one addiction to address. You *can* get two people into treatment at the same time, I've done it on several occasions. There are situations where doing a 'twofer' makes sense, such as with married couples or a brother and sister. I do not, however, *ever* recommend placing two closely-related people onto the same property.

Many programs have more than one location and, while I think it's fine to get two people into the same type of program, having those two people in two different physical locations may prove vital to their success. This is because, although it may seem easier to start a program together as a couple or as siblings, it can be just as easy to leave the program together when those two people are having a bad day *on the same day*. It happens, so if you find yourself in this position, don't allow that couple, brother and sister or boyfriend/girlfriend to talk you into sending them to the same property if it can possibly be avoided.

Later that day, after being hired by Karen and with Baxter at my side, I head my PT Cruiser up Interstate 5 to the Grapevine, then over to 99.

Karen meets me at the door of a large, ranch-style bungalow on the edge of town. It's late afternoon and the hot, dry air is pleasantly invigorating after the hazy, ozone stench of the Los Angeles basin.

Karen invites us into her living room where her husband John is sitting on a large sectional couch with Karen's mother Lori.

Baxter, tail wagging, runs past me and immediately hits it off with everyone.

My eyes confirm what I had suspected. Lori is a prisoner of the same kinds of medications her daughter is on. As Karen introduces us, Lori sits listlessly on the couch, barely focusing her attention on me before receding into the dream world she has fashioned for herself. She is heavyset, with the swollen and discolored ankles of the diabetic. Her walker is positioned within easy reach. I guess she is in her late seventies, but it turns out she is in her fifties.

John is in a polo shirt, stone washed jeans and loafers and has an easy manner. He recently graduated from medical school and grants me the same courtesy he would any professional.

Two teenage girls are sitting off by themselves. Karen introduces one as Lisa's daughter April and the other as her own daughter Joyce.

April's hair is roughly cut and dyed jet black. Her features, although quite fine, are heavily accentuated with lurid, purple eye shadow, black kohl eyeliner, mascara, black lipstick and a nose ring. She has on black leggings and a black T-shirt studded with paste diamonds. Bare feet with black nail polish complete the effect.

Joyce, by comparison, has the shiny, slightly chubby good looks of an adolescent girl about to flower into womanhood. She's not into Goth like her overly pierced cousin and is probably on track for a comfortable life as a suburban professional.

Lisa's husband Mike is there as well. He shakes my hand loosely but doesn't say anything beyond a cursory "hullo." He is a tall, heavily-built guy with a shaved head, an earring, and a tattoo on his left bicep. He is dressed in a well-worn T-shirt, jeans and brand new work boots.

The patriarch of this little clan, Gus is slouching comfortably in an armchair. When it's his turn to be introduced, he stands and clasps my hand in a firm, hail-fellow-well-met handshake. He looks directly into my eyes as though to take my measure, so I take his.

His skin is pinkish white and has the heavy, leathery, wrinkled texture of a long-time smoker. His eyes are a pale cornflower blue, rimmed with sandy-colored lashes and topped with bushy gray eyebrows that need trimming. White whiskers enclose his lips which spread wide open every time he grins, exposing dark red gums studded with very few and very crooked yellow teeth.

Gus, come to find out, is an honest-to-god mountain man from Virginia. He has a thick, Appalachian accent and appreciates a good joke, especially his own, which are numerous, obscene and punctuated by loud guffaws. He served in the armed forces for 35 years and has been an alcoholic for 50. He delivers the information with such temerity, I wonder which of the two accomplishments he's prouder of.

These are the main players, but I have yet to meet Lisa.

I begin to talk about the intervention process but don't get very far before loud assertions about how Lisa lacks discipline erupt from Gus's armchair.

"No one ever offered *me* a trip to a resort! My daddy would have just taken us out back—and you know what happened there!"

No, I don't, nor do I wish to. Baxter seems to like Gus, however, and bounds up on his lap, distracting him from his tirade and giving me the opportunity to continue briefing the others.

Although Gus comes across as a caricature of an ornery old cuss, I keep my eye on him as having real value in making the intervention a success. My initial thoughts are if he will agree to a script and stick to it, a caring and loving offer from him—one without any qualms—might have a great impact on Lisa by simply being so out of character. On the other hand, too long a leash on this guy could turn him into a real pit bull, with considerable potential to mess things up.

I suggest that Mike, Lisa's husband, introduce her to me so I can tell her about the program. After that, the family will gather and read the letters they had prepared. The letters would enumerate the reasons why everyone loves Lisa and say they would miss her being part of the family and why. After reading the letters, the family will unanimously ask her to enroll in a program in San Diego. They will also outline the attractiveness of the program, starting with the beautiful facilities, the swimming pool and sauna, the fact there would be no psychiatric drugs (a big selling point for her family), and no forced confessions. It will be presented as a chance for her to recover and reintroduce herself to a life without drugs.

I decide the best course of action is a standard intervention structure in which everyone will write a letter to Lisa, read it aloud and then, as a group, ask her to accept their offer of help and to at least give treatment a try.

I also prepare the family for the eventuality of Lisa saying "no," in which case there will be more steps to plan, but for now making the offer of help to Lisa in an organized way and without confrontation is the only thing I want to concentrate on.

Hope for the best and plan for the worst; that's the basic rule. I plan for every eventuality I can think of based on the addict's character description. "*What if...?*" is the index. *What if* she blows out of here? *What if* she says she wants to think about it? *What if* she says "yes" a more complicated proposition than one might think. *What if* she locks herself in her room and won't come out? You must have sufficient answers to these kinds of questions before going into the first meeting with your addict. Otherwise, you'll lose control when the chips are down and find yourself unprepared in a fumble.

Interventions are 90% preparation and 10% execution. Remember that, and your chances of success will increase exponentially.

Karen, Mike and Gus, as expected, ask questions and are involved in the briefing from the beginning. Although Lisa's daughter April doesn't have much to say, she telegraphs her involvement with an occasional nod of her head to her aunt and uncle.

As we talk and a specific plan for Lisa begins to emerge in my mind, I realize Lisa's husband Mike hasn't said a word the entire meeting. Not one. Even Lori, medicated as she is, has contributed to the creation of a plan. In my experience, an unknown quantity is not necessarily a safe quantity; I need to know exactly where Mike stands.

"Mike, I need to take Baxter out for a short walk. Why don't you come with us?"

"Sure, Man, no problem."

Once outside, I ask him point blank, "So what do you think, Mike? Do you agree Lisa needs this?"

"Hey, it *is* okay with me, Man. I know she needs help. I want her to get help, I do (I believe him), but they just laid this on me last night. I had no idea they were going to take Lisa into rehab."

He had no idea "they" were going to do the intervention, not "we." He agrees Lisa needs treatment but apparently, feels left out of the family discussions. This is his wife but, in his mind, he has little or nothing to do with the intervention. This is *their* thing; he sees himself supporting Lisa in whatever *she* decides to do.

210

This is not good because what if she says she *doesn't* want to go? Will he agree with that? The whole intervention might go south if he did; it would be *the two* of them against the family.

In Mike's defense, he really didn't know about it until that same day and he therefore feels little responsibility for it. By the same token, as Lisa's husband he has potential veto power and can pull the plug on the whole thing.

"If it's going to be like that television show, she will never go. She watches the show. I can tell you, Dude, I can write a letter and do that stuff myself, but I didn't because I know she'll never go for it." *(And, I thought, you don't want to be the bad guy.)*

It's never easy.

A question occurs to me: "Mike, how is she *buying* these pills if she's stuck at her house and drunk every day by noon?"

He stops and looks at me, puzzled. "Oh, I figured you knew," he continues, "She gets them from Lori."

From *Lori*??

I read his face as I try to clarify, "Are you telling me her *mother* gives her all those pills?"

"Yeah," he answers, obviously embarrassed. "Crazy, right?"

Wow, I thought. And this isn't just a few pills to help with a sprained wrist. Lori is giving her daughter lethal doses of illegal prescription medication.

I just need to continue the intervention and get Lisa into the program *regardless* of where or how she's getting her supply, but now I have to handle an on-site drug supplier who also happens to be her mother.

I wonder if Karen knows. I figure she must since I became privy to the information so quickly. In my mind, I immediately forgive her even if she does. I can't imagine how humiliating it must be to know that your own mother is providing drugs to your sister and putting her life in danger. All of these issues, however, are Pandora's boxes, and I already have enough to deal with. In any event, I have to get Mike involved to make sure things go smoothly.

If there's anything I've learned, it's that you can't force a person to do what *you* think you need them to do. If you try, you'll not only lose their trust but you might also tank the whole intervention. Based on this, I do occasionally take a leap of faith.

Here is a guy who is *not* happy his wife is drinking and abusing pain medications. He wants to be a part of the intervention, as long as he remains free to do it his way. I ask him how *he* feels the intervention should go.

"You can read your letters but *I* know what she will or won't agree to. I can take her into the garage after you read the letters, and… I'll get her to agree to go."

Conceptually, I have no problem with what he's saying.

"Mike, I just want to make sure she doesn't make an emotional hostage of you in that garage."

"No, no, no. That's not going to happen," he insists earnestly, "She's not going to do that to me. Besides, she needs the help."

"All right, But I want you to agree if you are in the garage with her for more than 20 minutes without some kind of communication to me about what's happening, I'm sending in the troops."

I have no idea what that means but, at the very least, I need an anchor point. That way, if things get squirrelly, I have his okay to interrupt. Besides, he seems genuinely convinced he can get Lisa to agree. It *would* make my job easier. It would also create something priceless in any intervention – a sense of self-determinism and control on the parts of both Mike *and* Lisa.

"You won't need to do that. I'll let you know what's happening." He seems almost cheerful in his response.

That said, I have the same radar as anyone else in terms of a sense of people. John, Lori, and Gus did all speak highly of Mike. According to them, he's honoring the provisions of his parole, holding down a job and staying out of trouble.

A guy on felony parole who is actively working to get his life together is actually not a bad bet. He strikes me as being genuine and *he has a lot to lose*, so I make the decision to trust him. Besides, if I exclude him, I'd have a problem for sure. He would have every justification to turn on me and kill the intervention.

Given the choice, I decide to gamble on a healthy horse with a bad history.

We go back inside and I begin going over the plan, which is now a solid sequence in my mind. The challenge is to get it to *happen*.

At this point, Gus begins butting in about getting the intervention "done and over with!" I step on the brakes as necessary, but it takes some skill to fashion a complete plan while coping with Gus's "hurry up and finish."

Gus's behavior is very common in interventions. It's understandable people want to get it over with and get to the other side, but *it's very dangerous to rush*. Remember, if you fumble the ball and find yourself without a contingency plan for what occurs, you'll be right back where you started. You not only have to pick your battles carefully, but you also have to plan them thoroughly–*without* rushing.

Gus is laying it on thick. He does have one valid point, however. If Lisa begins drinking, it will extend the time needed to get through the intervention by another day. All things considered, however, adding time is the least of my worries.

Gus is now complaining about needing a nap. (*Spare me.*)

"Listen, Gus, I understand your concern. It's late. If you need to go home and lie down, by all means do, and we'll do the intervention tomorrow."

"No, that's okay. Better get it over with." He quiets down.

"We really need to work out the plan first, so by all means stay, but nothing is going to happen with Lisa until we have gone over every aspect of how we are going to get this thing to work. Okay?"

"Okay."

I go through the steps with the family one more time and tell them Mike is going to go in ahead. Gus, Joyce and I will be waiting outside. Mike will signal us if Lisa is sober. If not, we'll wait the extra day.

This is an important point: You can't go through an intervention with the added chaos of someone who's drunk. I've done interventions and certainly have met with more than my share of people who were stoned or a little buzzed, but generally speaking, I don't meet with people who are falling down drunk unless I think I can get them into the car and driven to the program. Apparently, when Lisa hits the bottle, she quickly goes off the rails.

Add in the meds she was taking, and you might as well be talking to an armchair.

We all go over to Lisa's house and, after a few moments, Mike comes out and waves us into the garage.

Aside from the smell, which is a repellant mix of dirty ashtrays, stale beer, unwashed clothing and rotting food, the conditions in the garage are slightly worse than I have expected.

Unfinished sheet rock lines one of the walls. There's a hot plate and other kitchen paraphernalia scattered along a countertop that lines the back wall. The floor is unfinished cement. Open closets and shelving have been fashioned along part of the wall farthest from the door. Most of the clothing, however, has been dumped on the big double bed right in the center of the space, and buried somewhere beneath that huge jumble of clothing and bedding is Lisa.

Mike is sitting on a wooden chair near what, I assume, is the head of the bed. The look he gives me is so proprietary that I begin to understand how much he wants this intervention to go right and how he wants the control necessary to make sure it goes right. It also strikes me he genuinely loves whoever is buried beneath that pile of laundry.

His tone with her is deferential. He asks her if it will be alright for me come in and speak to her. Apparently she agrees. He helps her to into a sitting position on the bed so we can talk more as equals than as patient/practitioner.

As the mass of clothing falls to one side, I see Lisa, who, as could be expected, has the doughy obesity characteristic of a person who has been hooked on multiple prescription drugs for a long time. Nevertheless, she is remarkably tuned in.

Mike relinquishes his chair to me and, as agreed, leaves the garage.

I introduce myself and ask her forgiveness for the intrusion, putting the onus for my presence on her family.

"No problem," she says without looking at me. I move from the chair and perch myself on the edge of the bed. I begin telling her about my own struggle with painkillers (a personal history with just about every drug has definite advantages in my line of work).

I'm rhapsodizing about my love affair with Vicodin when the dam bursts. Lisa tears up and exhales hard. I continue with my story. I tell her about my failed relationships, my struggle with life, my love affairs with other drugs and my numerous attempts at treatment. I tell her about the program her family has chosen for her. I describe everything that's positive about the treatment center: the food, the individualized care, the swimming pool, the freedoms of it.

The golden rule is: *Always* pitch aesthetics. Even the prospect of helpful therapy doesn't sell tickets nearly as well. I also make it clear to her this is *not* an attempt by her family to ship her off and assure her they'll be there for her every step of the way.

Lisa abruptly agrees she needs to clean up her act, but can't do it now—because of her daughter April, because Christmas is just around the corner, and because her husband is just getting back into a normal life. I acknowledge her fears but do not discuss them, and then tell her that her family has something to say to her and is waiting for her in the living room.

She gets up and, without a battle, walks into the house.

Lisa sits down, and Joyce immediately begins reading her letter. Then Lisa's daughter April breezes in from the kitchen, as planned. Her hands, tipped with black-lacquered fingernails, do not hold a letter, but she sits down next to her mother as she was instructed to, and grabs her hand. I watch, optimistically, as Lisa grabs back.

After Joyce, the rest of the clan read their letters to Lisa, who maintains a very stoic expression throughout, ending with Gus. Obviously, she is inured to her family. It's evident whatever they think of her situation, she will not be easily moved by anything they say.

I chime in after Gus finishes his letter, which is remarkably civil. "You know, I think all they're asking you to do is give this thing a *try*."

Mike, however, is already moving.

"Listen, Babe, everyone has said what they needed to say, and I want to talk with you privately, okay?" Mike stands up and offers his hand to Lisa. She lets go of her daughter's, takes his, and follows him to the garage.

I'm always a *little* nervous, but this is a bit different. All my latent fears about Mike suddenly well up inside me with a gut-wrenching enumeration of the things that might go wrong. What if he isn't clean? What if he's on the run right now and they're packing their bags? What if, what if, what if...

I step outside and quietly take in deep breaths of the crisp, cold air. It had this quality to it, like there's nothing in it. There is only empty air. I find it strangely comforting, like there is room in the universe for anything, including enormous risk.

Before his twenty minutes expire, Mike comes out of the garage and asks, "Is tomorrow morning okay? Like 6:00 a.m.?"

I think I see a halo over his head. But, we are far from being out of the woods. "Yeah, fine," I say "Great. 6 a.m. it is."

I duck into the garage to confirm with Lisa this is a good time. "Yes, tomorrow morning early is totally fine."

I don't get much sleep and spend most of the night lying on the hotel bed, half-watching the television, running over every possible scenario that might interfere with Lisa entering the program. The intervention has gone extraordinarily well so far—maybe *too* well. I'm paid to worry, to plan and to keep planning for every contingency until I drop the addict off at the treatment facility. And I do. It's all I do. If this happens, we'll do that; if she does that, then we'll do this, *ad infinitum*.

At 5:30 the next morning, I back my car up to the garage door and walk into the house. Everyone is up or arriving to say goodbye. I speak briefly with April over breakfast in the kitchen. She is bummed her mother won't be home this Christmas. I see through the purple and the real shadows under her eyes and grasp something of the strain she is under. I remember adults preaching to me when I was a kid, so I don't say much. I just listen to her talk about how she's planning to have Christmas with her family despite her mother's absence. She'll be all right. Thanks to her stepdad and the intervention, she'll have many other Christmases with her mother when her mother will *be* her mother, not a drugged facsimile.

At 6:00 a.m. Mike and Lisa emerge from the garage, and I thankfully let go of the long list of contingencies I worried about overnight. Karen, Lori, John and Gus gather around her to say their goodbyes, which are protracted but tearful and very heartfelt. Finally, Mike gives her a hug and a long kiss and helps her into the passenger seat of my car.

As we cruise down the freeway, Lisa opens up to me a little about her habit. She rattles off the names of anti-depressants, anti-psychotics, painkillers and other drugs like a pharmacist. She speaks with self-loathing of her "weakness" and how much she envies people who lead "normal" lives. She resents that she isn't ruled by the circadian rhythms of night and day, but rather by the rhythm of uppers and downers, the use of which governs when she sleeps and when she is awake. She can remember what life was like before her own slide into addiction began which, she says, started with a prescription for Vicodin after her appendectomy. Most frustrating to her is watching her sister's family gaining wealth and influence as they grow older while her own life is just a confusion of losses, unrealities and hallucinations. She has not worked in almost seven years and every day is consuming enough narcotic to kill a large animal.

We eat a second breakfast at McDonalds at the foot of the Grapevine. Ninety minutes later we are in San Diego. I drop her off at the detox, and that is pretty much it. Baxter and I drive off together and head for the grocery store. I never have steak when I get hired, only when I succeed. Maybe that's one of the reasons why Baxter, who never turns down a little bit of steak, does his best to help.

Lessons from Lisa

First, I think any book on addiction should include the damages often wreaked by prescription medicines because, tragically, in recent decades, the popularity of psychoactive drugs, sleep meds, anti-anxiety and anti-psychotics has created a whole new class of addict: people addicted to drugs which allegedly, are not addictive.

The fact is one can buy some form or another of OxyContin in just about any city in any state across our country. For whatever reason, this is not attributed to Big Pharma and the companies which actually produce the drug and profit from this situation, so we need to take responsibility for it ourselves because these drugs are highly addictive, and overdoses from OxyContin alone outpaced overdoses from cocaine and heroin combined years ago.

When Karen called me, she felt the intervention would be next to impossible to do but, once we got going, we came to find out it wasn't. This is the case with many interventions. In fact, it wasn't nearly as difficult as everyone was afraid it might be. Most families just need to get *going* when it comes to doing an intervention and stop coming up with reasons why it might not work. Just put your heads together with the determination to make it work!

When interventions fail, it's usually for one of three reasons: It never gets off the ground—there is a lack of thorough planning, or the family gives up too soon.

If you need to do an intervention, remember the words of Mark Twain. "The secret of getting ahead is getting *started*."

Sarah

The call is from Irvington, Oregon, an affluent 'boom burg' on the other side of the Willamette River from Portland. The tone of the woman on the line is flat, almost bored, as though she's told the story a thousand times before, but *what* she is telling me sends a chill down my spine. She's describing her niece, "...she has her own house, about $2,000,000 in cash in the bank and she's free-basing cocaine out of a bong."

Yikes.

Certain situations worry me more than others. Some are more dangerous, often life-threatening for the addict. Others present challenges, unknowns and things that seem impossible to overcome. This situation worries me for all these reasons.

Two people, the young woman and her male cousin, are in this together and have millions of dollars in cash to keep them going for a long time, or long enough to kill them.

Here's a little background on the chemistry involved. First, cocaine is derived from the coca plant, native to South America. Cocaine causes increased levels of dopamine and stimulates pleasure and movement centers in the brain. "Free-base" is a solid form of cocaine which has been re-purified, typically using baking soda, water, and a little heat. "Crack" is essentially free-base but with other chemicals, fillers and stimulants added to it and refers to what is sold on the street.

Cocaine is arguably one of the most physically addictive drugs, right up there with heroin. Although it does create a psychoactive effect like methamphetamine, it is also an anesthetic and analgesic. It causes sleep deprivation and creates paranoia, sometimes severe and dangerous. Freebasers often have auditory hallucinations such as hearing people outside the door, police sirens, people shuffling around under their beds, hiding in their closets and so on, as well as symptoms such as rapid speech, severe vitamin deficiencies, and dehydration, all of which make them jittery and paranoid.

A bong intensifies the drug's effects by producing a strong "lung hit" on the part of the user. Imagine taking a deep breath right before you go underwater. Now imagine that someone puts a lit pipe in your mouth and asks you to do it again. That's the kind of inhale a freebaser takes, and the smoke is pure cocaine. Because the water in the bong cools the smoke, the freebaser can take a much *bigger* hit than he could get from a regular pipe.

Now, back to Sarah.

Sarah and her cousin Matthew are closer to each other than they are to their own brothers and sisters, "too close" according to some family members. Both of their families want to hire me, but I decide to work primarily with Sarah's mother, Martha.

Matthew's brothers and parents have already attempted to get him into treatment. Their failed effort involved trying to strong-arm him into a car, the result being he no longer trusts them (of course). Sarah, on the other hand, is by all accounts still on good terms with her mother, who seems like the best route to establish contact with them both.

Martha lives in a mansion on a vast property in a beautiful part of Oregon. She has a soft, southern drawl that reminds me of Dolly

Parton. Her manner is sweetly feminine, and her concern for her daughter is evident in her frank responses to my questions.

I meet Sarah's brothers who are solicitous of their mother but, unfortunately, neither is close to Sarah.

Martha eventually drives me to Sarah's home, a lovely, two-story brick house with white-trimmed gables and a steeply-pitched roof. It's set back from the road behind an expansive but neglected garden.

Sarah answers the door. She appears to be about thirty years old and is extremely obese and unkempt. Her features are obscured by the doughy puffiness typical of a long-time drug user. "Mom! What are you doing here?" She does not look at me, concentrating intently on her mother's face.

"Sarah, this is Steve Bruno. I met him while looking for a way to help you out of this hole you've dug for yourself. He has some suggestions he'd like to share with you. I know this is unexpected, but I was wondering if you would come have dinner with us."

"Now?" Adrenaline is the dominant molecule.

"Yes, dear."

Sarah does not invite us into the house but leaves the door open as she disappears inside to get her things. Martha and I walk into the living room which is crowded with expensive, overstuffed furniture. Clothing, newspapers, and magazines are scattered everywhere. The rug is stained and pocked with burn holes, as are the couch and chairs, telltale signs of her habit.

Some time passes before Sarah reappears. She is nicely–even expensively–dressed, but her clothes are ill fitting and her overall aspect is slovenly. She obviously trusts her mother.

223

She doesn't question my presence, but simply smiles as we sit quietly in the car.

We don't say much until we arrive at the Chinese restaurant Sarah has recommended. Over dinner, I tell her the story of my experiences with freebasing, about the demons, my waking nightmares, the paranoia, the phantom police, the imaginary people I would hear shuffling back and forth behind closed doors.

I know I'm getting to her when she begins to lean forward in her chair, tears welling in her eyes. She keeps saying: "Yes, yes, I'm going through those same things." But whatever response she wants to make cannot be fully articulated. I can see a plea for help somewhere in her eyes.

She's a hostage no matter where she is.

"Your mother would like you to go to a program in Daytona Beach, Florida where you can get out of this mess you're in. Matthew's parents have also agreed to cover his costs should he decide to do a program as well. It would be great if you could do it together."

She doesn't seem particularly keen on the idea of continuing with Matthew. I can't imagine how difficult it is for her to be in an incestuous relationship while constantly high on cocaine.

"Yes, I want to go," she says, almost without hesitation.

This happens in a handful of interventions; the addict has essentially been waiting for rescue but hasn't known how to ask.

Sometimes families hire me without having first spoken with their addict because they have enough money to hire someone else to have that conversation *for* them. But this is not the case with Martha.

I already know that for the past several months she has tried, but has been unable, to get Sarah to come out of the house for longer than 10 or 20 minutes at a time.

"Great," I reply, "let's go tomorrow. We'll take you home, you can pack your bags, and I'll make the travel arrangements." Martha is looking at me intently. I do not return her gaze. I know the power of crack cocaine; I know its shackles; I know its pain. Sarah is in a prison. I am under no illusion this is going to be simple, or easy. I always like to give the addict the benefit of a doubt at first. It pays off when I have someone who owns his decision to go to treatment. It can make a big difference in his willingness to stay.

Whenever an addict agrees to go to treatment, I certainly *want* to believe it's true.

Dinner over and agreement ostensibly reached, I drive Sarah back to her home and then Martha to hers, where we book our plane reservations for 4:00 p.m. the following day.

When Martha and I knock on Sarah's door the next day to take her to the airport, however, instead of coming to the door, my cell phone rings. It's Sarah. As I stand outside her front door with her approximately three feet away, she presents a litany of excuses beginning with her state of mind. She explains she does not feel comfortable opening the door. I imagine a split screen shot with her just inside the door–sweating, nervous, paranoid–and me on the other side.

Obviously, we are not going to make the flight.

I do not challenge or berate her. She is high on coke which means she's already paranoid, so berating or being condescending to someone in that condition will make them *less* apt to communicate with you. "No problem, Sarah, why don't you go shopping and we'll talk about this again later."

About two hours later, after dropping Martha off at her house, I decide to check out a local gourmet market that Sarah had mentioned, extolling their prime rib sandwiches.

While browsing the bakery aisle, whom should I bump into but Sarah! There she is, as unkempt and paranoid as I'd imagined her earlier, pushing an overloaded shopping cart with what looks like about $600 worth of groceries in it. Matthew is behind her. I give her an easy-going greeting and introduce myself to Matthew.

He is a big-boned, hefty guy, his eyes reluctant to meet mine. I ask him if he's willing to talk. He says okay. I tell them I'll be at their house the next day.

The next afternoon, I arrive at Sarah's door as promised. Matthew answers and invites me into the living room where we sit across from each other. I tell Matthew I would like his help in getting Sarah to rehab. He agrees that Sarah needs to get off the dope even though it's obvious he's using just as much as she is.

I rapidly sketch out the details of the program with him—the beautiful, expansive facilities in Daytona Beach and its high success rate. Almost as an afterthought, I suggest maybe he would benefit from the program too.

"This would be a good time to go to Florida, get some sun, and handle this thing once and for all."

Matthew hunches forward in his chair. "Yeah," he replies, looking scolded. "I'm thinking about it."

Sarah comes in, joins the conversation, and, after conferring briefly with Matthew, tells me again she is willing to go. It's obvious if Sarah weren't in the equation, Matthew and I would probably not be speaking to each other.

We decide to have Sarah's brothers take care of the dogs. We book another flight, and Sarah assures me she will pack her bags.

The next day, however, when Martha and I arrive to pick her up, once again Sarah refuses to come out.

Sarah is adamant that she *does want to go* but she can't go...*yet*. She tells us she can't leave her dogs and must get them to a veterinarian. She stands in the doorway, shifting from one foot to the other, obviously aware what she is telling us doesn't hold a lot of water. Her eyes dart back and forth; her brow is glistening with sweat and her skin has the grayish, clammy look of a hard drug user. There is no question that she has been hitting that bong hard since the day before.

Martha says flatly to her daughter, "Sarah, *you are lying to us.* You have *no intention* of going to Daytona Beach." And then to me, "Go home Steve. This has been going on for a long time. She won't change." Sarah keeps looking down as she shifts back and forth in the doorway and says nothing.

In many interventions, there comes a time when the addict's stalling and failed promises overwhelm those trying to help. The family tells itself the intervention has failed when what has actually happened is the family has just given up too soon. This is where an interventionist can take over and carry the show. I include this intervention in this book to illustrate the frequent need for greater perseverance than a family may expect at the outset. In fact, perseverance is often *king*.

Sarah isn't fighting me, the drugs are fighting *her*, but her mother can't make that connection. To her, Sarah is lying. To me, Sarah is dying.

"Martha, if you're willing to continue to pay for my hotel room, I'll stay and continue to try to get Sarah on the plane. It's a fatal error to give up now," I explain, "Sarah has not become a bad person, but the drugs are certainly making her look like one—I'll give you that! To her, the prospect of going even one day without coke is almost unimaginable. It is to *anyone* hooked on it. But we *can* make this happen. You've already paid my fee. You can afford the hotel for a couple more days *more* than you can afford to risk losing your little girl. Just let me stay and do my work."

Martha's heartbreak is evident. On the outside, it seems like it doesn't matter to her anymore whether Sarah goes to treatment or not, but I know otherwise. She appears to be in a state of apathy. If I can get Sarah to the program, all will be well.

Two more days go by.

The scenario does not change: Sarah agrees to go. Sarah is not ready to go. Sarah does not go. Sarah agrees to go. Sarah is not ready to go. Sarah does not go. Plane reservations are made and canceled, remade and re-canceled.

On the fourth day, Sarah tells me, "Give me twenty minutes." Twenty minutes later, Sarah comes out and says, "Give me twenty minutes." (Translation: "I just need *a few more hits*.").

I have to come up with an idea. Both Sarah and Matthew are on a no-holds-barred freebase binge. Sarah is not moving. She's inhaling crack cocaine out of a bong for heaven's sake. Despite this, I have no doubt she *wants* to go. We just need to figure out *how* to do it.

I share an idea with Martha.

The next day, after another failed attempt to get Sarah to the car, Martha pulls some of her chemotherapy pain medication out of her pocket, takes her daughter's hand and says, "Sarah, I want you to take these." She gives her daughter two of the powerful painkillers.

Sarah looks at her mother and, sounding like a lost, little girl says, "I'm having a very hard time."

"I know, Sweetheart, I know." Both Sarah's and her mother's eyes are full of tears as Sarah takes the pills and brings her hand to her mouth.

We stand nervously in the doorway as Martha and I stall for time. Ten minutes go by. Eventually Sarah's hands hang limp in her mothers. Her eyelids begin to droop. We move quickly. We have to be across the country before she goes into withdrawal again.

"Sarah, get your dogs. Matthew, get Sarah's suitcases," which thankfully are packed and ready to go. I continue nudging for complete control of the situation, "Okay, everyone in the car. Matthew, why don't you grab your things and come with us."

He looks about as trustworthy as a cobra. Matthew cannot stay in the house now that Sarah is leaving. Matthew is her cousin but, at the same time, he's also a stranger here. The money is Sarah's, and the house and everything inside of it belongs to Sarah. All of it everything, *including* their crack habit, is paid for by Sarah. Matthew has nothing. Martha tells him she's already arranged to have the locksmith come to the house that evening and to have a cleaning crew come the next day.

The picture is clear: In a matter of minutes, Matthew is either going to be homeless or on his way to Daytona Beach.

This is my roll of the dice; I know Matthew will be left with nothing. I also know he feels that he's leaving a lot. He's had a life of easy money and easy drugs. There is something in his eyes that seems dangerous,, but I'm not about to let anything stop what's happening with our effort to save Sarah. I do not wait for an answer. I bundle him into the car along with Sarah, her mother, and the dogs, and peel out of there as quickly as I can before anyone has a chance to change his mind.

Matthew, whom I could see in the rearview mirror, looks furious. His eyes are shifting back and forth rapidly, and he's pressed about as far into the corner of the back seat as he can go. His hands are gripped tightly in his lap. His aspect is tense and wary. I do not try to speak to him, and I give Martha a warning glance to keep quiet too.

Martha commandeers the dogs and asks one of her sons to pick them up at the airport and take them directly to a veterinarian. I can't give them much of my focus, but I have a bad feeling about them.

An alert Skycap at the airport quickly assesses the situation with Sarah and offers a wheelchair which we gratefully accept. Sarah plops into it like a huge, snoring sack of cement. To his credit, Matthew continues to hold it together. With Sarah in the wheelchair nodding in and out of consciousness, we could excuse the motley condition of our crew by describing Sarah as being terminally ill and needing medical attention which she is on her way to Florida to get.

From the way things went that day, one could say, if you ever need to get through airport security quickly with a crack addict, give him a couple of painkillers, plop him into a wheelchair and then lie about everything. It seems to work.

When the plane arrives in Florida, Matthew is in observably worse condition than Sarah, who is still asleep as we roll out to the curb and get into a taxi. But we *have* all made it to Daytona Beach.

As it turns out, Matthew's parents prefer a different program than the one Sarah is going to, but they do each go to a program that will be at least five months in length.

My hunch about the dogs turns out to be correct. After being told some of the details of the dogs' recent history, they are diagnosed with acute drug withdrawal. The vet keeps them for several days and successfully detoxes them from crack cocaine. That must sound strange but remember those two dogs spent hours upon hours in a sealed, crack-smoke-filled bedroom for months on end. I'm not sure there are many interventionists who can say they not only did a double intervention successfully but that it included two canine addicts *as well*. Maybe I'm the first to have done a "crack *cocaine*" intervention!

When I saw Matthew a few months later, I barely recognized him except for his red hair. He had been working out and had dropped all the drug fat. He was muscular and fit and, by all appearances, was doing well. He even had a smile on his face to greet me.

Sarah went to a twelve-step program and graduated after six months. To my surprise and delight, she got a degree in drug counseling and eventually became the program director for a women's recovery program in Ft. Lauderdale, a silver lining indeed.

If I had gone home when Martha wanted me to, I don't know what would have happened to Sarah.

What made the difference between failure and success was *perseverance*.

There was also a belief that, at the end of the day, Sarah genuinely wanted help. She didn't want the life she was living, even though on a daily basis she seemed to want to do the drug more.

Lessons from Sarah

Among the many reasons I decided to include Sarah's story were her repeated promises to go to treatment, followed by her missing her flight *five times in a row*. It illustrates the importance of *perseverance* and *keeping a level head* even though things may not be going according to schedule. Things *rarely* go according to schedule during an intervention. If they do, you should consider yourself very lucky. If they don't, honestly, it's par for the course.

Perhaps the most common mistake families make is they stop "three feet from gold." Sarah's mom was ready to have me fly home after Sarah missed her second flight. If I had, Sarah would probably be dead. The reality is she didn't miss two flights, she missed five. And this illustrates why the family needs to be ready to push through whatever comes its way *for however long it takes,* within reason.

More importantly, Sarah's story shows that simply because an addict is telling you one thing and doing another does not necessarily mean his initial statements were delivered with the intent to deceive. Addiction makes liars out of us, so before you go around treating the addict like a five-year-old–scolding him, talking down to him, berating him for not following through–just remember that's the condition you are sending him to treatment to repair.

Lastly, Sarah shows us the incredible darkness she was putting herself and her family through, can be pierced by the bright light of recovery. Sarah has now helped thousands of women just like her, all because we insisted helping her was worth it.

Aaron

"You don't drown by falling into water. You only drown if you stay there."
~ Zig Ziglar

Working as an interventionist over the years has taught me drug addiction covers *all* demographics. It does not respect any social or economic borders. It has, without discrimination, permeated the ranks of the underprivileged and well-to-do achievers alike.

The first call from Aaron's mother came in two months ago. Padma Stevens is a professor of world literature. Aaron's father has a Ph.D. in astrophysics and teaches in that field. Neither of them, however, had any idea what to do about their 17-year-old son.

Padma found my website and contacted me, certain Aaron was using. At that moment, however, she said they didn't feel it was necessary to resort to an intervention and just asked me for some advice on what to look for, how to speak with her son about drug use and so on. I did my best.

If a family comes to me and isn't ready to do an intervention, I give them a reality check when they need one, but I don't spend a lot of time pushing. If a family agrees only because they feel pressured by me, then it becomes *my* intervention, not theirs. It's not necessary that *every* family member has to agree about the need for an intervention, but there should be a reasonable level of commitment; otherwise, when things get rough, family members tend to scurry off in all directions saying it wasn't their idea in the first place.

In the next call from Padma I learn that the scene has changed entirely.

"We need to do something about my son. It's gotten really bad."

"What is he doing *exactly*?"

"Well, he hardly ever comes home! He won't speak to his father or me and, when he does, it's only to demand money, the car, and gas. He's *very* abusive now and I'm afraid of him. I've come to dread when he comes home more than I dread when he's gone. His father simply wants to kick him out of the house. I don't know what to do."

I ask for more information about Aaron's habits and learn that, aside from the hostility, he doesn't seem to fit the profile of a drug user. He keeps a regular schedule. He goes to sleep at night, wakes up in the morning, eats with a good appetite, leaves the house and comes back at night. A meth addict is typically much more erratic, and opiate addicts sleep all the time, even nodding off at the table.

Aaron has been caught smoking weed but isn't exhibiting the behavior patterns of a habitual user of any hard street drugs, but it's also difficult to know for sure when your only information is what a parent tells you.

We decide I should drive from Hollywood to San Francisco so we can meet face-to-face.

The Stevens live in one of the city's stately Victorians in an upscale neighborhood. Mrs. Stevens meets me at the door. She is kind and soft-spoken, but her eyes are full of pain and worry. She invites me to sit down for a lovingly prepared breakfast of eggs, homemade bread and English tea.

Aaron is 17 and dependent on his parents for lodging, gas, food, clothing and pretty much everything. For a nanosecond, I'm tempted to go in with guns blazing and suggest they cut Aaron off immediately unless he agrees to go to rehab, but I don't.

Instead, I remind myself that approach rarely works and ask to meet Aaron.

After listening to his mother's muffled voice rise and fall from upstairs as she cajoles him into meeting with me, Aaron comes slouching down the stairs into the living room sporting a baseball cap with bill turned to the back, a faded T-shirt, and Tupac Shakur pants slung low, clinging to his thighs with the help of a wide leather belt. Black tennis shoes with a gold metallic Nike swoosh complete the ensemble. A scowl darkens his soft adolescent features. He definitely has the *gangsta wannabe* motif down cold.

"My mom wants me to talk to you. What do you want?"

"My name is Steve. You must be Aaron."

I offer my hand, which he takes without returning the pressure of my grip.

"Your parents are worried about you."

Aaron smirks. I continue by describing the rehab program. I gear my pitch to those aspects of the program I think might engage his interest like the fact it's a co-ed facility in Ohio which might be a good opportunity to get away from his folks for a while to sort out his priorities. When I finish, his response is brief.

"Thanks for coming by, Man." He turns and leaves.

This is not good. I suddenly have a hunch Aaron is into more than just smoking weed. He has neither the vulnerability of an addict, nor of someone innocent. His easy and self-assured hostility, combined with the fact he was not stoned when I met him, makes me suspect he is either dealing or is a gang member.

I meet with the parents and share my growing conviction that, in any case, an intervention *is* necessary. Aaron has definitely lost his way, and *whatever* he is into needs to be addressed. I agree their son's behavior is not normal for a young man with everything in life at his disposal and, although he seems sure of himself to the point of threatening those closest to him, the situation is in fact out of his control. We agree to start with a loving appeal.

I ask them both to write letters which they will bring to a meeting with Aaron and read. I tell them writing the letters will ensure they will be telling Aaron everything he needs to hear.

Mrs. Stevens writes a beautiful letter. In it, she tells Aaron how much and why she loves him. She says he is smart, strong, good-looking, creative, adept with computers, and has a lot of potential for a very rewarding life. She says she misses him and the times they used to get together just to talk. But these days, the only communications she receives from him are demands for money.

Aaron does not oppose the meeting and listens as his parents read their letters. They make their appeal to him to go to the program. They are very convincing in their wish for him to take them up on their offer. His response is eerily like the one he gave me at our first encounter: polite, emotionless and final.

"Yeah, I get what you're saying," and nothing more.

This is not a good sign. The guys who are throwing dishes at their parents, banging their heads against the floor, punching holes in the wall, and crashing their cars into telephone poles are all *engaged*, if only in protest. Aaron appears to have no connection at all.

I conclude we must play this game on Aaron's turf, tough and to the point. After we meet with Aaron, I advise the Stevens to apply for a restraining order which, if issued, will have the power to forcibly remove Aaron and ostensibly the threat of retaliation he had been using to dominate them. To get a restraining order issued, however, they must convince a judge that Aaron is a threat.

I ask Mrs. Stevens to think of any incidents during which Aaron threatened her physical safety or her life. This is difficult for her to do for her because it is against her gentle, loving nature, but I reiterate to her that a restraining order–with consequences–is a way we can impose control on Aaron and make his choices much more real to him.

The judge has no problem issuing the restraining order. When Mrs. Stevens confides in me that she is afraid that Aaron might actually burn the house down, I advise her to hire a private security guard to serve the order to Aaron. I explain I can't do it because I have to be "the good guy" offering a way out.

Aaron doesn't strike me as a heavy hitter though, even if he is in a gang. He has no tattoos, no colors, and none of the telltale signs of a real insider.

Aaron does, however, have a computer-authorized, encoded key to one of the family cars, a black Infinity. Mr. Stevens doesn't know how to disable the code, so they buy a Club for the steering wheel.

The security guard arrives at the house. We talk about the details of the plan while he installs the Club on the car. Then, he walks upstairs and, in a very businesslike manner, serves Aaron with the restraining order. The response is immediate, *"F**K OFF!"* Aaron yells, hurling the order back at the security guard. He then rounds on his mother, screaming, "I am going to *kill you*!" and runs out of the house to the car.

Much to our despair, the security guard mistakenly left the Club *unlocked!* Aaron throws the now useless security device from the car and drives away, tires squealing and horn blaring.

Great, I think to myself. *Now he has the car _and_ an increased sense of power.*

Not exactly the effect I was going for, but succeeding in an intervention is often the result of being able to regroup and move forward with a new plan, as opposed to giving up simply because one part of your existing plan goes south. It's bound to happen. If you count on it, when things do go south (which they invariably will), you don't have to go south with them.

Mrs. Stevens is reduced to heaving sobs, refusing the comfort offered to her by her husband. Following my advice, Mr. Stevens calls the police and asks them to charge his son with grand theft auto. I figure the best place to address Aaron will be in a jailhouse where we will have some cards to play, but the police tell Mr. Stevens they can't comply. If Aaron has had prior permission to use the car, the best the police can do is charge him with *using a vehicle without permission,* which carries with it no force of pursuit. After carefully re-reading the restraining order, however, we realize the judge *has* prohibited use of the car, so we still have a shot if we can find Aaron *with* the car.

As things stand, Aaron doesn't seem likely to return to the house and will probably spend the night sleeping in the car. Mrs. Stevens tells me that Aaron often hangs out in the college parking lot where she works, and she thinks she knows the location of one of his main drug suppliers, or so she thinks.

We search for hours with no result but, early the next morning as I'm driving through the college campus where Mrs. Stevens teaches, I spot the Infinity *way* in the back of the parking lot. I can't tell if Aaron is in the car and wonder for a minute if he might be armed (it seems like the kind of stupid thing a kid might do), but because using the car is prohibited in the restraining order, he can be arrested for contempt of court anyway, so I call the campus police.

An officer goes over and examines the car, but Aaron is not there. I sit there for 45 minutes with the cop, telling him who I am and that I'm trying to get Aaron to treatment. The officer tells me if Aaron shows up and gets into the car, he *will* have to arrest him.

"Well," I reply, "arresting Aaron won't solve anything, but getting him to the rehab program will. If he loses this car, he has nowhere to go. He has nothing, no game, nothing. That'll give us a better chance to get him into the program."

While we talk, we look through the car. There are shreds of marijuana everywhere, particularly in the trunk. It looks like the car has been used to transport *a lot* of weed.

That's enough for the officer. He calls in a tow truck and, while the Infinity is being pulled onto the truck bed, who should come walking around the corner but Aaron himself! The officer turns to me. "What do you want me to do, Steve?"

"I want Aaron to walk away without the car."

"Okay, I think I can do that" he says, turning toward Aaron. "Are you Aaron?" he asks.

"Yeah, why?" Aaron is on the defensive.

"Just come over here, I want to talk to you for a second." The officer is wearing a campus uniform which includes shorts and a short sleeve shirt, so Aaron must assume he's a rent-a-cop.

"No, Man. I'm not talking to you."

"Aaron, you need to stop and talk to me."

"F**k you, I ain't talking to you."

"You need to stop walking," the officer commands, no longer asking, "and listen to what I'm saying."

Aaron pulls out a gold chain, puts it on, crosses his arms, and says, "I am not talking to you." Despite the seriousness of the situation, I almost laugh. Then Aaron lunges at the Infinity. The cop grabs him. Now holding him by the arm, the cop says once again, "Aaron, I just need to talk to you."

You have to give the cop credit for keeping such a level head.

I jump in. "Aaron, talk to him. He's not going to mess with you if you talk to him."

Aaron wriggles, pulls himself free and starts walking away, saying to me, "This guy's not gonna mess with me."

The cop gets in front of him, grabs him *again* and says, "You just need to stand still."

Aaron starts struggling, but this time the cop says flatly, "Okay, I can't do this."

He twirls Aaron around, slams him on the hood of the Infinity, handcuffs and arrests him.

In a few minutes, I find myself watching Aaron being driven off in the back of a police cruiser.

Great.

Well...at least I know where he'll *be* for the next day or two.

I go back to the house to deliver the news but his mother already looks defeated. She tells me Aaron called from jail saying, "Get me the f**k out of here!" and again threatened to burn the house down.

I have no way of contacting him unless he calls us back, so I wait.

About 9:00 p.m., the phone rings, and I answer this time. Static breaks apart a woman's voice; it sounds as if she's calling from some distant overseas location, *and* she's the most bored person on the planet, asking if I would accept the charges for a collect call. I accept. After a series of clicks, Aaron's indignation permeates the distance.

"What are *you* doing over there?" He says, more as an accusation than a question.

"You are freaking your parents out, Man. You cannot keep doing this." Aaron tells me he wants to get bailed out. His bond is $15,000, which is $1,500 out of pocket to the bondsman.

When his parents refuse to pay unless he goes to Ohio, he gets off the phone and then apparently calls his dealer for a loan. He tells him he is owed $700 from his job at college, which he can collect and pay back right away. That turns out to be a fatal error because what Aaron himself *doesn't* know is the job is really a *volunteer* position and his mother—who works at the college—has been the one paying him!

The dealer fronts the $1,500 so Aaron gets out of jail to find he has no home, no car AND no money to pay his dealer back which is, of course, an enormous problem. He either has to renege on the agreement with his dealer or make a deal with us. A few hours later we are once again on the phone together. I tell him, "Look, if you get on the plane to Ohio, your parents will pay off the dealer."

The line is silent for a few moments.

"Ok," he says, "but I'm not staying."

"Fine," I say, matching his tone, "but it's straight to the airport. *That's* the deal." He tries to argue with me about it and wants to get the dealer paid off before we go to the airport, but I stand my ground.

Aaron says nothing on the way to the airport. In fact, he says nothing more to me at all. He does, however, get on the plane. The last I heard he made it to Ohio and, after about four or five weeks, made some friends there and started doing the program in earnest.

Lesson's from Aaron

I include this story because most of you are going to be dealing with someone who's acting unreasonably, or even crazy at times.

You'll notice Aaron's outbursts and violence were mainly directed at his mother, not toward his father much and not much toward me. While it's true he was rude toward me, his real hostility was directed at his mother who was the key, the pivotal component in almost any major family decision. His addiction had taught him that in order to survive, he needed to keep her paralyzed in a state of panic or hopelessness.

This is a perfect example of an addict targeting the person he deems to be the force behind the intervention and trying to drive that person into a state of fright or despair to stop the intervention from even taking place. Addicts like Aaron are a lot like that lizard in Jurassic Park that shot ink and flared out its fins when it felt threatened. It's an effort at controlling someone by convincing them they cannot win, no matter what. But Aaron's case is *also* a perfect example of the fact the fight *can* be won if you stay calm and turn each situation to your advantage as it arises.

Aaron's story also illustrates the fact that if your addict gets arrested during the intervention, it can work in your favor, depending on the situation. In Aaron's case, we made a deal to bail him out as long as he was willing to go directly to the program.

No matter what happened with Aaron, his family and I kept the intervention moving by continually regrouping and being willing to let go of one plan and create a new one as we went.

Sherrie

"There is a lot of suffering in the world.
There is also a lot of overcoming it."
~ Helen Keller

Watsonville is a little afterthought of a town midway between Salinas and Santa Cruz, along the central California coast. Purely agricultural, it boasts a billion dollars a year in strawberry exports, including some very good locally made pies. It's a nice place to live, and I did for a few years with my little dog Baxter.

One day in early autumn I get a request to do a "transport" which, simple though it may sound, is more often than not its own kind of adventure.

Transports straddle the line between helping an addict who is willing to go to treatment and having to stage a full-blown intervention. They are done when a person is willing to go to treatment but, for whatever reason, needs to be accompanied.

The person I am to transport is a 35-year-old female who has just been released from jail. She was charged with alcohol-related felony child neglect. Her family in Arizona is wealthy and willing to pay to have a professional transport her. Her aunt tells me Sherrie will be waiting for me in the parking lot at the Auburn jail where she has been held.

Auburn is in the foothills of the Sierra Nevada, so I pile some supplies and a happy little Baxter into my car and head north on Highway 80.

I pull up to the jailhouse about 5:00 p.m. They roll up the sidewalks early in Auburn, California and the place is deserted except for an attractive, tall blond woman dressed in jeans and a blazer standing all alone in the parking lot.

Introductions are brief. Her name is Sherrie, my name is Steve, this is Baxter whom I'm holding in my arms; he's glad to have the extra company. Sherrie is indifferent, looking at neither of us and in the unmistakable tone of the privileged says, "Okay, so I guess you're my driver. Let's go."

She ungraciously gets into the car and accepts Baxter on her lap without comment or emotion. He is flowing cuteness exponentially in her direction with obvious expectations of an affectionate rubdown in return. It never comes. Sherrie stares blankly out the window, sipping from a commuter cup. She chain-smokes and fiddles with the stereo between sips. After a few minutes, in addition to smoke, the unmistakable smell of alcohol registers in my nose. The fact I can identify it means she must be drinking it straight. Her eyes are half closed and her head is bobbing back and forth in the seat.

She must have walked to the liquor store and then *back* to the jail parking lot.

Great! I never tire of the moments I myself am swindled, having swindled those around me for so long!

I pull over to get a better look at her, call my contact at the program and tell him the reason for our delay, I'm sure they won't accept her in this condition since there is no on-site detox.

"Get the booze away from her. Feed her. Slow down... Enjoy the scenery. You have a long drive ahead of you anyway, so give her time to sober up." Why did I even call? I could have given a thousand other excuses. Night surrounds us. I cut way back on the accelerator. Sherrie stops complaining about me taking her coffee mug and starts to complain about the reduction in speed and then falls asleep mid-sentence, her head knocking gently against the window. She soon starts thrashing around, in and out of consciousness.

There's no scenery now. The road is just a road, every mile exactly like the last. The pavement looks as if it was poured the week before. Illuminated by the halogen headlights, the yellow lines are almost too bright to look at.

She was sober when I picked her up so I figure she isn't in any immediate danger other than the possibility of vomiting all over my dashboard, a minor risk compared to other hells I've found myself in, so I roll on. Baxter finally gets fed up and leaves her lap for more stable accommodations in the back seat.

After about an hour of meandering down the dark, deserted country highway we arrive in Roseville, a good distance from where we have to end up. Sherrie startles awake and slurs at me with some urgency that she has to pee; I pull into the parking lot of a Walgreen's. Fortunately, at this hour, the store is deserted. Only a curious cashier and I are there to watch her stumble down the aisle to the bathroom.

She emerges a few minutes later and stands silently, trying to locate herself as she slowly sways back and forth. Then, with obvious effort, she looks around, frozen in a myopic gaze as I watch in horror as she falls *straight back* as if she's been shot in the head point blank.

Her reaction time could probably have been measured in hours. I hear a "SMACK!" as the back of her head hits the linoleum floor.

"Sh**!" I exclaim as I run over to her. No one hears me. The store is *thankfully*, empty except for the cashier. Blood starts pooling onto the floor by the time I reach her side. Lifting her, I see a gash on the back of her head with hair clumped around it. I grab some bandages off the shelf, tear them out of the packaging and start staunching the flow. "Is she okay?" asks the clerk, appearing suddenly behind me.

"Obviously not. Can you please just ring up the bandages?" Sherrie is semi-conscious as I throw down a few dollars on the counter and let her lean heavily on me as I make our way out to the car. I see Baxter, paws on the rear window, watching us with sudden, avid interest from behind the small spot of fog he'd made on the window, his little head cocked to one side.

Once Sherrie is buckled into the front seat I start to call 9-1-1, but Sherrie–suddenly coherent–grabs me with both arms and tries to manage a yell but emits a coarse, loud gasp instead. "No, Steve, please! No hospitals! *No cops*!"

"Look," I tell her, matter-of-factly, "you cut your head. You *have* to go to a hospital."

Her eyes are now wide open and, for the first time, she looks directly into mine. She pleads softly with me, "Steve, Steve, I do not *want* to go to the hospital. I do not want to go to the *cops*."

Real fear has made her alert and coherent. My choices? Drag her to the hospital where she will probably bolt, get arrested again for violating the terms of her probation (in which case she'd *never* get to see her children), or I can handle this myself, accept the liability involved, and get her to the program where there will be a nurse and a team instead of just me.

250

"Alright..." I say, looking her straight in the eyes, "but if you pass out, I am taking you to a hospital, with or without your permission."

"I want some coffee. That will help."

"No Sherrie, it *won't*. No coffee. And do *NOT* fall asleep." I decide to get off the road to give her a chance to get cleaned up and me a chance to regroup and to make sure the remainder of our trip is as uneventful as possible. I pull into a hotel and get a room.

A small knot has formed at the back of Sherrie's head. The gash isn't that big but has bled profusely as head wounds tend to do. I clean it up and bandage it as best I can. She tells me she needs clothes and makeup. She obviously didn't bring luggage to jail with her. Her clothing is rancid with alcoholic sweat, her blazer streaked with blood. New stuff would do a lot for her morale.

I run a bath for her and, while she's cleaning up, I step outside and call her aunt. She gives me the okay to buy whatever Sherrie says she needs. When I go back into the room, there's a handwritten list waiting for me on the bed which includes bras, underwear, a dress, a tracksuit, and makeup. I spend a few moments ruminating over the benefits of a career change before deciding to comply. I decide to leave her on her own in the hotel room. There is nowhere for her to go, and even if she were willing to come with me, I have no confidence in her level of sobriety.

Sherrie is walking a thin line, but I figure the least destructive route is to give her some time and space and handle the shopping myself. I wait for her to finish her bath and then make sure she is awake and that her head has stopped bleeding completely.

Then I make my way down the street.

Thanksgiving is days away, so the stores at the local mall are open late, which is fortunate for me since it's already a little after 9:00. I head into Macy's and lean heavily on the sales staff to do my shopping for me.

When I get back, the bathroom door is closed, but I can hear Sherrie shuffling around inside. I lay the purchases out on the bed, then go to the door. "Look, Sherrie, we have to go. I am going to go outside. Get dressed, ok?"

She mumbles that she hears me.

A long fifteen minutes go by before I go back into the hotel room. Some of the clothes and the makeup are gone and the bathroom door is shut.

Almost home free, I thought (knock on wood). I lie down on the bed and start reading Gideon's Bible while waiting for her to emerge from the bathroom...

And emerge she does—naked!

Wha-?

She launches herself on top of me, wraps her legs around mine, and begins kissing my neck with considerable enthusiasm.

Oooh man!

I would like to note here that Sherrie is a cute, 35 year-old who, alcoholic or not, is more attractive with her clothes off. What can I say? We live in hedonistic times. Man-Steve and Interventionist-Steve wage a silent but mighty philosophical war before I push her gently aside.

I am fully aware of the fact she is willing to propitiate me with sex and the consequences of her doing so would be disastrous to her future state of mind, as well as a finish to my career.

I tell her that, although I dearly want to take her up on her offer, it would be a breach of ethics for me to do so. Then I tell her that after a few weeks, once she qualifies for a pass, I'll come and get her, buy her a dress, take her to dinner and a show, and after we'll get a nice room and have all the jungle sex we want.

None of this would ever come true. I know it, and the reality that I am lying to cover rejecting her sinks into Sherrie like a long, slow blade. Maybe I overshot it, or she just knows. Either way, it doesn't matter. The expression on her face becomes one of utter self-loathing (not exactly the effect I was going for). She slides to the foot of the bed, away from me, and begins sobbing, her head buried in her arms. Deep, heaving sobs. I'm still clutching the Bible in one hand. *God*, I call silently, *I could use a little help here.*

And, there it is.

As if on cue, Baxter jumps onto the bed and begins nudging Sherrie with his nose, wagging his tail and licking the tears from her face as if he can love away her sadness. She looks at him, gathers him deeply into her arms and begins rocking and sobbing, half laughing at his completely disarming affection. Like he was saying, "If Steve won't cuddle with you, *I will!*"

I'm no expert on a woman's body language but can comprehend that my little dog Baxter had – in that moment – managed to salvage an otherwise impossible situation.

Hallelujah. Praise Baxter.

After a few minutes, Sherrie sets Baxter carefully aside (to his disappointment), and wraps herself in the comforter from the bed. She stands up and says matter-of-factly, "OK, let's go."

I don't even have to coax her to get dressed. She still looks teary-eyed, ashamed and embarrassed but takes several moments of happy consolation in all the makeup I have purchased for her. Soon, with some artistic skill on her part and a little patience on mine, she looks more than presentable.

I order some take-out which she eats with appetite and then she sleeps for two hours until she feels and looks like a human being again.

Eight hours from when we started, we're on the road again.

The cold, deep indigo of night is relieved by the cold, solid grays of early morning as we finally arrive in Watsonville. We begin the drive up Gaffey Road, a long winding strip of asphalt leading to the top of Mount Madonna and a beautiful 35-acre treatment campus. Mike, my contact, meets us outside and says, "Hey, we can't take her. She has a cut on her head and needs to go to the hospital right now."

"Great, have fun!" I reply, and start walking in the opposite direction. "I have gone *beyond*. She's sober. If she'd been willing to go to a hospital, believe me, that is the first place we would have gone."

Mike regards me for a few seconds and then walks back in.

I'm on my way down the stairs when he comes running out after me. "Steve! Sherrie won't go to the hospital with anyone but you. Please take her and get her checked out. Make sure she hasn't cracked her skull. If the doctor says she's okay, we'll enroll her."

How can I say no? This will be our second date.

While we wait in the emergency room, I handle Sherrie's relatively minor hangover thirst with lots of lemonade from the vending machine and by taking her on frequent cigarette breaks. When she's admitted, the orderly looks at the cut on her head and tells her they'll probably have to cut her hair.

Sherrie is on the verge of refusing care by the time the doctor comes in. She shoots me a murderous look. I take him to the side and explain enough for him to get the picture. The doctor gives Sherrie's head a thorough exam, bandages her wound, but leaves her hair alone. She smiles broadly at me. He gives us the "all clear" and I drive Sherrie back up the mountain. Outside, we hug awkwardly. She looks down and then walks into the center. I do not expect to see her again.

Two weeks later, I'm back at Mount Madonna delivering someone else at the end of another crazy story. I'm walking up the front stairs when I look over to where the sun is beaming down through the trees and the spring mist. There are blooms bordering the path. I see a beautiful woman, the sun back-lighting her hair, walking along the path, stooping now and then to pick flowers. I think to myself, *wouldn't it be nice if Sherrie could be like that one day?*

Just then the woman looks up, and – there she is! WOW! I knew I liked this program for some reason!

Walking down the path, the sun at her back, comes a magically transformed Sherrie! All the tragedy that had marred her beautiful face was gone. She looks intensely feminine and healthy after only a couple of weeks of walks in the sunshine, vitamins, good food and fresh, coastal mountain air.

She glances up, immediately recognizes me and walks over. Her greeting is shy, almost silent. I'm thrilled by her transformation and tell her she looks great, which she does. There is no doubt she's happy to see me, but the events of that drive from Auburn still stand between us. I congratulate her on her good health and her progress. Then she softly and shyly says she has to go, or she'll be late for her class.

Lessons from Sherrie

If you wonder why I do what I do and how I can endure a road trip like that like it's just another day at the office, it's for the moments which I find utterly blissful, like when Sherrie refused to go to the hospital with anybody but me despite how things started between us. Then of course there was the day I saw her a couple of weeks after she arrived, doing so well and regaining her life. Someone did it for me, and now I'm able to do it for others like Sherrie.

After writing this, a friend asked me if I was crazy to include a story like this. "It's all over the map," he said. Aren't you supposed to be writing the book to sell the idea that interventions are *easy*?"

My answer? *Absolutely not.*

I'm not telling you these stories to pitch you something that isn't real. If an interventionist tells you the process is easy, then he's either inexperienced or you're being sold a bill of goods.

I succeed because I'm realistic about what the work consists of. Sometimes I get a simple, A-to-B intervention but that's the exception, not the rule. It's usually a controlled mess at best.

The rule is: Be prepared for anything and be grateful if most of it doesn't happen.

Sherrie's story tells you to remain calm, and to keep things moving forward if things go to Hell in a handbasket. There is almost always a solution, no matter what the problem, but you must be able to maintain a level head and think it through. I may not always do what people expect. I do what I think will work, though, and that's how you win.

257

William

The humidity is tolerable this time of year in the south, as Winter loosens her grip in response to the warm breath of Spring. The smell of fresh cut hay and newly laid fertilizer is heavy in the air.

Somewhere amid this postcard-perfect landscape of farms, Baptist churches, old red barns and verdant green pastures is a 70-year-old tobacco farmer and the reason I'm in rural Kentucky.

William's daughter Collette called me the week before and, in a carefully controlled voice, described her once proud father as a man who, for over a year, has been ravaged by a crack cocaine addiction. He is now completely isolated from the family, his health in ruins, his fortune gone, his farms abandoned.

According to Collette, he has been "holed up" for the past ten months in his farmhouse which rests on what was once 900 acres producing soybeans and tobacco. Now, 200 untended cattle and a glass pipe are his only company, most of his farmland completely overgrown.

Collette first became aware of the problem when William didn't plant on time and, since the family doesn't live together and measures its contact by the seasons, the timeline for the cocaine to take hold has been as long as a year. In short, William is a 70-year-old man who has been smoking crack all day, *every* day for a year before anyone realized what was happening.

Because of this isolation, the details of William's descent into addiction are sketchy, and Collette isn't that forthcoming.

After some coaxing, I learn that Collette's brother, William's youngest, has been addicted to crack for years, and William hired him and a few of his friends to work the farm the year before.

William is a drinking man, and I'm guessing that, while William was imbibing, and in what I imagine was a combination of drinking and dares one late night on his farm, his own son convinced him to try the drug. And here we are a year later, addressing the most unlikely sort of person one thinks of when one thinks of a crack addict. But his condition is no different than that of any other crack addict. He is lost to himself and is almost lost to his family.

People who have never used crack have extraordinary difficulty understanding it only takes one or two hits to create an addict.

Personally, I find the endless debate on the character and moral fiber of addicts to be tiresome, pointless, and of no use whatsoever other than to make the person doing the evaluating feel superior, or to justify why confronting the problem is either beyond their ability or below their station.

Many people who are severely critical of addicts have no first-hand experience with it or, if they do, they have taken up soap-boxing about it. The continued use of drugs damages character, can make a reprobate of the most pious among us, and is a scenario I have witnessed too many times. It can happen to the best of us. William is a perfect example.

He holds title to three separate farms and hundreds of acres in what is one of the most productive farming areas in the state.

Soybean crops rotate with tobacco. William's children are all successful farmers, all except the son who led his father into the addiction. The others have homes and land that are vintage Americana.

Collette is a robust, 35-year-old woman, thickset and solidly attractive. She has the high color and healthy good looks of a woman used to hard, physical work. Her father's situation is a source of deep sorrow and puzzlement to her. She has no experience with street drugs except as something *other* people do in *other* places in the world—not her family and, not in a million years, her own father! It may as well be a story of fiction about another world in another part of the universe. But it isn't.

I meet first with Collette and then with the rest of the family: her sister, their husbands and William's parents, both of whom are in their nineties but are still sharp as whips and who maintain surprisingly high spirits about the intervention. Collette's brother is not present or mentioned, other than to enlighten me on his culpability. He is apparently on the run from local authorities for some petty crime or another, and the family has no idea where he is. I have no use for him in the intervention anyway so I let it go at that.

I shake hands all around, give a brief introduction of my credentials as, among other things, an ex-crack addict, and with it an explanation about my purpose and methodology as an interventionist.

My first concern is to meet with William and to assess his situation for myself. Collette offers to drive me and make introductions so William won't immediately try to shut me out. He still loves his daughters, of this I am certain. I don't have to meet him to know that going out there with Collette will be money in the bank.

After a short drive through some of the most beautiful farmland one could ever hope to see, we arrive at William's house. Collette comments on how dilapidated the trucks parked out in front look, "so much worse" than when she was here before.

They do look pretty beaten up but, when I get closer, I realize they aren't. They've simply been abandoned for months on end. The field is overgrown with weeds and shrubs, some of which are securely rooted in the wheel wells and engine compartments, seemingly intent upon never letting those vehicles move again. For her part, Collette focuses on reaching the front door and doesn't even glance at the vast expanse of vines taking over the surrounding fields and curling along the fence, mindless of our approach.

The house itself looks as if time has stopped on its doorstep. There is no visible movement; even the air seems unnaturally still as we approach the front door.

Rusted hinges screech loudly in protest as Collette opens the screen. She slams the brass knocker against the front door. No response. Then again, *BANG BANG BANG,* before realizing the door is unlocked. She pushes it open slightly and whispers, "Daddy?" It wrings my heart as she says it a second time, her voice wavering.

Looking over her shoulder, I see into a dark room. The smell of cigarettes and stale beer punctures my nose as the warm, damp, musty air from inside–eager for escape–suddenly washes over us.

The misfits from some far-off urban core who use the drug called *crack* have now reached her own family and have taken away her beloved father, leaving an evil with which–left to her own–she is clearly unable to cope. After hesitating a moment, she enters the room. I follow, ready for anything.

262

We walk into the dark, haze-filled room. At the opposite end, facing us is an immense, pink body lying motionless on a couch, as if an enormous sea elephant has been dumped there. I half expect the smell of rotting flesh to assault my nose. Thankfully, it does not. The body looks bigger than the couch, and may be; I estimate William's weight is close to 400 pounds.

Collette's voice is a thick whisper. "Are you smoking in here?" she jibes, attempting to be playful, her voice halting like a little girl trying to be friendly to a wounded pit bull that used to be her friend, hoping the dog will lick her hand and not bite it.

I've seen some gnarly situations in my time, but I'm surprised at the wreckage I see here. It smells like a damp ashtray and old beer, but there is something else–a medicinal odor combined with feces, like a badly-managed assisted living facility.

The curtains are drawn against any sunlight filtering in, casting the room in perpetual twilight.

William James Warren, a 70-year old, third-generation tobacco and soybean farmer is sprawled on the couch in front of us, clad only in a pair of yellowed jockey shorts and a dirty, gray baseball cap.

Two years earlier he could do the work of three, younger men. Now, grotesquely obese, his pinkish-yellow skin stretched tightly over his swollen abdomen, William has almost been killed by his own hand.

His face is overgrown with a beard that looks like the vines overtaking his farm. I make out two small, gray eyes underneath the baseball cap looking back at us, seemingly in shock, like embers of fear, or rage, I'm not certain which.

William makes no attempt to conceal himself or to cover his near nakedness. The wooden framed sofa sags heavily under his weight. It might as well be a hammock.

Upon closer inspection, I realize William looks quite ill. His face is pale and haggard, his massive torso is bloated and rubbed raw in places, and he has rashes on both legs. Peeling skin hangs down both shins.

I can see Collette's concern on her face. How can anyone *help* someone in such a condition? Having a physician assess his physical condition must wait. I still have no idea what his state of mind is, so that's first on my list.

Collette and I stand there for a minute before I start by apologizing for the intrusion, as planned. This is my standard method of first contact. Being apologetic can be disarming and gives the other person a sense of having the upper hand.

Collette walks over, kneels as if to pray with him, and gently takes William's hand. He recoils abruptly.

We're suddenly on the defensive, not knowing what to expect, not knowing how to respond. Collette nervously offers to take him to the bathroom while I stammer out an offer to leave.

Collette and I had agreed beforehand that if things got sticky with William, we would just exit and regroup. William, however, doesn't seem to have heard either one of us, so I stay put. Then, just as suddenly, William lurches forward and, with obvious effort, heaves his great bulk up from the couch and, as if he hadn't walked upright for days, waddles awkwardly across the room, down three steps to the bathroom, and disappears inside, ignoring us completely. He re-emerges a few minutes later, climbs back up into the living room and eases himself onto the couch in a half sitting position. He stares at me in what looks like disbelief, then looks away.

I speak again, deliberately apologetic, propitiating, trying to grant William some sense of control over the situation. This is his house; I am the intruder; his retaining a sense of control is important.

"I know this is awkward," I start. "It is for me, too, actually. You probably don't want anyone here, much less a stranger, but I *do* have some experience with some things you might relate to, and I told your family I would come over and talk with you. So how 'bout if I just talk for a few minutes, and then I'll leave. You don't have to say anything."

William doesn't object, but he's looking back at me as if he expects me to attack him instead, so I sit down without approaching him too closely. I mumble an additional apology for the intrusion, justifying my being there as the result of some real concern on the part of his family.

I ask Collette if she will step outside while William and I talk. Once she's gone, and without preamble, I segue into my story.

Over the next fifteen minutes, I replay to William a summary of *my* experience with crack. I tell him about coming down from the drug one morning just as the sun was rising, my arms sore, my hands red and deeply creased from *hours* of holding an imaginary door closed to keep out "heard and felt but unseen intruders." *And* down *another* three hundred dollars.

Why did I insist on spending so much money, only to have a horror movie installed in my mind again and again? After, I would drink, *a lot*, to ease the paranoia, then to sleep, and then…to forget. And forget I would– because I would do *exactly the same thing* the next day.

At no time is William giving me any sign he's even listening.

Like a grotesque, weathered, fallen statue, his immense body lies sideways toward me, motionless. Only his eyes are fixed in my direction from across some incalculable distance.

I talk about details only a crack addict can appreciate—details about my struggles, my depression, my incredible highs and ruinous losses. Most importantly, I share how I eventually got *out* by going to a program like the one his family is now offering him. I tell him how reluctant and cynical I was when my family approached me, but also how my decision to go and at least *try* helped me regain my family, my self-respect—*my life*.

The main hope of his family lies in the possibility I will get William to agree to go the program during this first meeting, but I'm not paid to be optimistic.

The *effective* intervention lies in one's ability to gracefully work *around* certain factors and get the addict to the front doors of the facility *no matter what, and* in as good shape and with as much self-determination as possible.

All families *want* to achieve this, but for most, there are just too many histories, minefields, personal payoffs and agendas that make the intervention into some form of self-run group therapy layered into a disaster. In addition, families tend to over-analyze their situation which is, in fact, a natural and normal condition. This is another reason I suggest hiring a professional if possible.

Moving on. One of the great mistakes families make is to address the addict as if he can be reasoned with. I'm not saying all addicts are insane. This is a confounding irony to most people since, on the surface many addicts seem quite self-aware, and in many ways they are.

However, in just as many ways they are not. This is important to understand, to face and to acknowledge.

The addict's overall condition tends to elude *his own* understanding because his attention is on his circumstances or the drugs and alcohol as the cause of his problems, as opposed to the fact that he has lost his way in life and no longer makes decisions according to what was once his conscience.

The neighborhood into which one must venture to achieve a successful intervention, therefore, is that of the addict, not the other way around.

Families tear their hair out trying to get their loved ones to listen to reason, when what they need to be focused on – and stay focused on – is getting the person through the front door of the treatment center, even if you (the family) must *abandon reason* as part of the process to get the person there.

It is because of this that an intervention is, more or less, a manipulation.

I get up to leave, but I can see a question appear suddenly in Williams eyes. *Aren't you here to try to help me do this thing you're asking?*

The look he gives me is unmistakable.

My hesitation on going too fast turns out to be an incorrect assumption on my part. To William, I'm going too slowly.

Gently and gingerly, I suggest the door is open if he would *happen* to be interested in going to a *beautiful* facility in southern Arizona. Here comes the pitch: I tell him it's a resort property just down the road from an 18-hole golf course on 80 acres. It even has its own little lake.

The picture of the place I paint for him is all true because it's important not to misrepresent the facility. It may be tempting to exaggerate while describing the facility the family has picked out, but it also gives the addict a reason to call you out on it and back out upon arrival. It's best to focus on *real aesthetics*. You can do it. *Make* the place sound appealing, but don't embellish *too* much.

Families need to keep this sales technique in mind. In fact, many families would benefit quite markedly in their efforts if they were to brush up on basic salesmanship.

I assure William if he'll go and just give it a *try*, he can always leave. *This is something every addict needs to hear but which very few family members can say easily.* Whether or not you say it, it's true—so you may as well use it to your advantage.

I make the place sound nice and tell him whatever he decides is fine with me. *I'm just there to help.* I talk for about five minutes *just* about his daughters, how much they miss him, how much they love him and how much they want him to say "yes" to this offer of help. I tell him how hopeful his parents are. I finish with some remarks about the potential loss, or rebirth, of his farms.

"But whatever," I add. "It's your life."

I want William to trust me. If I can get him to reach *back* it will be a good start. I move my bishop: "I promised you I'd split, so I'm going to split."

The more one can get addicts to reach *back*, the more it reinforces their self-determination to accept the offer of their own accord and the more ownership they will have while at the program.

Getting up to leave is a good example of a way to get someone to reach *back*. Of course, this needs to be premeditated following the conclusion it might actually work. I had decided it might in William's case.

As I stand up, William stops me with a loud, sharp grumble. He manages to retch out two dry words, "you know..." he croaks, as if he hasn't used his voice in weeks, or months.

He obviously has no idea what to say. His few words fall, disappear and become a heavy silence.

I try a rescue. "Yes, William, I *do know* what you're going through. I know what it's like. I do. And the fact is, I'm here because I said 'yes' to a similar offer one day way back when, and now I'm sitting here and am not in such bad shape."

I make it simple, "Look, just say 'yes,' and *I'll* take care of the details. I won't let anything bad happen. I'll keep you informed of every detail as we go. No surprises. I promise."

A minute goes by, then two.

He finally sits up on the couch, then looks at the floor, which is littered with beer and whiskey bottles. Each one contains a few smelly, wet cigarette butts. William looks like a behemoth surrounded and subdued by captors of his own creation.

He looks up at me and kind of surprisingly decisively says, "Okay." Then he heaves himself, belly first, into a standing position, teeters slightly, and waddles off to the bathroom again, stumbling slightly with each step.

Collette is stunned when I tell her of her father's agreement. She can't believe it. Fine with me. No matter how good things may look for a minute, I'm not paid to believe. I'm paid to achieve. I'm under no illusion we are anywhere but *just* getting things started. In what direction? We'll soon find out.

One could say an intervention is like driving a complex system of roads. When you find yourself lost or going down an unfamiliar road, *you simply have to find your way back*. The worst thing to do is to panic. The best way to find your way back is to prepare for getting lost in the first place. *Expect it. Plan for it. <u>How</u> might you get lost? <u>How</u> <u>can you get back</u> from that particular situation? What's another way you might get lost? How will you get back from that?* And so on.

Further, while getting an addict to agreement is *something*, it's *not* the same as getting the addict to pack his things, arrive at check-in or load himself into the car, and actually *arrive* at treatment.

When I was using, I would agree to anything you wanted if it meant you'd leave me alone. When and if your loved one does agree to go to the program, however–if you can help yourself–don't give him any indication you don't believe him. That, too, is a mistake. Too many families do this out of habit when interacting with a family member. It's understandable; just don't do it. On the other hand, you don't want to relax into gullibility either.

It's always a tricky balance and can be difficult. Expect it to be unwieldy and difficult *and* stressful, and for it to take longer than you hoped, then you won't be disappointed.

Collette finds some nasty looking crutches in the back of one of the pickups but which make walking for William quite a bit more tolerable. We manage to get William dressed, packed, out of the house, through the yard, and to the car.

I call to ask the intake counselor if he wants me to take William to a hospital in Arizona as a precautionary measure. He tells me no and says they will assess him.

As I mentioned earlier, William did end up having very serious medical conditions. The real miracle of the intervention, as it turned out, was the fact that, if we had not acted when we did, William would have been dead, possibly within days or weeks. It was *also* a good idea to get William to the facility since the *whole picture* needed to be addressed at once, *especially* the addiction. Until that took place, William would exist in the swamp he had created and his ailments would be a *greater* risk.

Last-minute flight arrangements are made. Thankfully, William has prescription painkillers. I am not a proponent of *unnecessary* drug use, but one must pick one's battles, and, if William is under a slight haze while we travel, it will make the trip a whole lot smoother for us both.

It's worth mentioning that, as an ex addict, I have never been under any illusion that simply because a person agrees to go to treatment, they are going to stop using right then and there. In fact, quite the contrary is typically true. Sometimes the *only* way to get a person to make the trip is to let them use along the way. I try not to know about it and, if I were to write about all the adventures I've had with individuals under various influences, I would undoubtedly be inviting legal problems.

My professional philosophy is there is no room to boast about adherence to the strictest professional ethics if you're doing it at the expense of an addict's life. What is the value of a worthless ethical stance? That is *my* professional philosophy. Other interventionists have theirs, but for me there isn't a debate.

Collette is *visibly* concerned. Her father is now miraculously going into treatment but packing hydrocodone in his luggage! He isn't popping any pills at the moment though and is not visibly under their influence, so I comfort her with the fact he is indeed going to treatment.

I'm rolling a lot of dice. I usually do, but I don't slow down during a winning streak. My mission is to get William to treatment where he'll be supervised and properly brought down. I have no interest in changing his status quo, only in getting him to a facility that can.

People on drugs are to a greater or lesser degree in a psychotic state, so reasoning with a person in that condition can be fruitless.

Reason does not work unless you have a knack for abandoning it. Planning your moves along the lines of the addict's thinking–his needs, his wants, exploiting his weaknesses *and* strengths–*this* is the thinking you must adopt if you are to succeed.

Giving the addict an attainable, short-term goal such as arriving at the facility works. Rambling on about how much he needs to go does not. Gentle simplicities work. Harsh measures do not. Complex deceptions *can* work but only if immaculately planned and objectively directed. Luckily with William, the crack just hasn't been giving him that lovin' feelin' anymore so, despite the challenges, we have that working in our favor.

As it turns out, William has not been on an airplane since the 60's, so the first thing he does after settling into his seat (his two seats actually –he can't fit into just one) is to light a cigarette.

So there he is, smoking on the airplane not realizing smoking on planes has been banned for years. I watch, mortified, from two seats back, praying he doesn't get us thrown off or arrested.

A young and sassy, black stewardess immediately shows up. (Keep in mind William grew up with a white dominant mindset.) The stewardess grabs the cigarette unceremoniously from his mouth and abruptly walks off. William gapes after her with a look of utter disbelief. What happened to the society he used to know? He sits there for a minute and then decides to light another smoke. I'm sitting two rows back and one aisle over so I have a perfect view.

The stewardess walks back up and is now standing behind him but right in front of me, mulling over what to do.

She handles the situation brilliantly. She takes out her own pack of smokes, walks over to William with a cigarette in her hand, and asks him for a light. He hands over his lighter. Without warning, she takes his *new* cigarette from his mouth, and before strutting off with his lighter says, "Now *stop* lighting cigarettes on my plane!"

If he were physically able to, I'm sure *William* would have *a fit.*

After two nicotine-free hours in the air, William looks like he's going to explode if he doesn't have a cigarette. We have a one-hour layover at Chicago's O'Hare airport, so I commandeer a wheelchair and set out for the front door, a 20-minute walk/run through a *vast* expanse of departure gates and shops. William has his cigarette and, in the sprint getting back to our gate, I'm pretty sure I qualified for the Olympic 800-meter wheelchair push. William is happily oblivious to my discomfort, but I don't mind. The fact we are on our way is the only motivation I need.

While driving to rehab from the airport, William tells me he's thirsty so I pull into the next convenience store we come to and shepherd him in.

While I buy him a Slurpee, he ambles to the back of the store, locates a hand sink (not *in* the bathroom, but just outside and right in the line of sight of the cashier), proceeds to pull up his shirt, unzip his pants and urinate into the sink. I keep my poker face on and distract the clerk by asking for change for a dollar while William completes his task. I get him out of there as fast as I can. The *last* thing I need is for him to get a citation for urinating in public, a half-mile from the facility. If this kind of thing happens to you, don't worry about it. Just keep moving.

As we drive into the big, sweeping, curved driveway, the facility, partly shrouded in nighttime fog, appears like a floating city in front of us.

Lights from the expansive entryway glisten in the evening darkness. Above the palatial facility I could see a thousand, different stars in the deep blackness of the sky,

We've made it.

After days of working to bring William to this point, it all seems to have taken place somewhere else and in a different time. We look up to see an attractive female intake counselor smiling as she walks down to greet us. (Hey, sometimes that's all it takes!) She opens William's door, beaming at him as if he were her best friend whom she's happy to see again.

William gets up from his seat as best he can and stands facing her. He has a big smile on his face as the woman takes his arm and helps him through the front doors of the main building.

There is no parade except for the brief hello and goodbye from the woman who escorts William inside.

That is the last I see of him and, as abruptly as it is a beginning for him, it is an ending for me.

I call Collette later that evening and tell her we have arrived safely.

She can't believe the intervention had *worked*. None of her family can either. If there had been a betting pool, I could have become a rich man. There are very few words between us at that point but very few are needed.

Several days later, I call the program and ask about him. They tell me his medical condition was critical. The peeling shreds of skin on his legs were not rashes, but gangrene. His bloated abdomen was edema due to imminent liver and kidney failure, and he had become incontinent shortly after arriving. The facility transferred William to a hospital. Collette is, nonetheless, happy to hear from me and tells me he would have died alone in that miserable house had we not gotten him out of there. She is genuinely relieved he is receiving real care for the first time since his introduction to crack.

As for William, he confessed to Collette he knew he didn't have much time left and had just been waiting to die when we knocked on his door that day. He told her he accepted my offer of help because he didn't want to die alone in that house.

Last I heard, two years after delivering him that fateful night, he had gotten his health partly back and was doing well.

Lesson's from William

Drug addiction is not the result of diminished moral fiber. William was as moral and solid as the day is long. No matter how pious your beliefs, or how well-educated you are or your age or socio-economic status, *no one* is exempt from addiction.

Also, never underestimate the possibility the drug or alcohol *itself* will hand the addict over to you, mid-intervention: the result of overuse, a drug-related fight or circumstance, or maybe just good timing combined with a bad hangover! It happens, so always think *opportunistically*. Take advantage of circumstances. Seek to create them. And don't stop planning after executing *one* plan – KEEP PLANNING as you go, as needed, *whenever needed*. Planning is *never* a bad idea.

Also, if possible, each meeting should have a definitive sweep: a beginning, a middle and an end. This is simply a matter of spending the time to plan *as you go*, to knock ideas around, to debate, argue and, if you can prevent those arguments from separating you, you and yours can come up with *real, workable solutions* for just about anything. I promise.

In the end, the *only* thing that matters is to get the addict's clothing packed, get him to the front door of the treatment facility, have him reach out his hand, grab the handle and walk through. Everything else, literally *everything else*, then becomes irrelevant.

The goal of an intervention is not to simply get agreement from the addict. The goal of an intervention is to get the addict <u>to</u> the program.

Jared

"It's a lot like wrestling a gorilla.
You don't quit when you're tired. You quit when the gorilla is tired."
~ Daniel Boorstein

It's mid-afternoon when we arrive at the opulent home of the subject of my next intervention. Sunlight hits the backs of Jared's father and mother, one of his sisters and me as his father knocks on the large wooden door of the not-so-well-maintained mansion nestled deep in the Hollywood Hills.

A minute later, standing barefoot before us, is the ultimate motivation behind the Mexican Drug Wars, the tunnels that link warehouses in Tijuana to San Diego, the anonymous corpses littering the Sonoran Desert, and the endless human caravans with their burdens of marijuana, brown heroin, and cocaine snaking their way north to Nogales, Arizona. He is wrapped in a fluffy velour bathrobe, his stubbly face segueing rapidly from surprise to a barely artificial, ascetic social grace as he surveys the scene before him.

"Jared!" cries his father, stepping forward and enfolding his beloved son in a firm embrace, then withdrawing to grasp his son's hand and gaze delightedly into his eyes. The answering stare is none too steady and lasts only a moment before shifting to a point just slightly above his father's left shoulder and directly at me.

"Hug your mother! And your sister!" urges Jared's father, caught up in this impromptu family reunion and oblivious to any hint of protest, as his wife Winny and daughter Cindy each in turn step forward to kiss and embrace the prodigal son.

"Debbie couldn't make it?" asks Jared, dryly, almost bored, still eying me suspiciously.

"Well, no, she couldn't."

Jared makes the first move. "And who are you?" This query is delivered so much like that of Lewis Carroll's hookah-smoking caterpillar that, for a moment, I imagine Jared atop a toadstool blowing celluloid smoke in my face.

"Steve Bruno," I answer, extending my hand. "You must be Jared. Pleased to meet you. Sorry for dropping in like this. Your family asked me to tag along. Could you and I have a moment alone? That way, I can get out of here and let you guys catch up."

His hand in mine is thin-boned and clammy. The pressure is aggressive, delivered with the authority conferred upon him as one of Hollywood's anointed. I take no offense. He is about to have his face removed, and his handshake tells me he has some inkling of that fact. Nevertheless, he nods to my invitation and ushers us into his house while his mother babbles on about how well he looks and how proud everyone is of him.

Off to a great start, I think to myself. Mom's already forgotten everything we talked about earlier.

This is often the case with moms. I've found one must be patient while moms shift from thinking about their son (or daughter) as an addict, to confronting it, and then being able to act on it differently than they have before.

The living room is a vast, sunken affair, a few steps down from the main foyer, sparsely furnished in the style of an Ivy League fraternity house: big screen plasma TV, the well-stocked entertainment center, bean bag chairs, the Italian leather sofa and loveseat combo, armchairs and a huge glass coffee table supported by an enormous burl wood pedestal. Everything is expensive. Nothing matches. Curtains flanking a big bay window pool onto the floor. Track lighting is on full even though it's the middle of the day. Undisguised surround-sound speakers are in awkward attendance. An enormous Andy Warhol print conspicuously dominates one wall, and the remains of last night's take-out are scattered across the table and onto part of the floor.

The three family members settle themselves around the coffee table. Jared scoops up what's left of last night's meal as best he can and then disappears into the kitchen. A minute later, he returns with a bag of potato chips and, without flourish, dumps it into a plastic bowl and plops the bowl on the table with an uncomfortable *BANG*.

"There are drinks in the bar," he says, waving toward an alcove against the far wall. "Help yourselves." Then, turning to me, "Will the patio out back do?"

"Yes, fine. Great."

He leads me out past the kitchen and dining room through patio doors to a flagstone terrace overlooking a canyon. I steer Jared away from the patio table and select two chairs out of view from inside the house. I arrange them so we are seated not directly facing each other but in the manner of two close friends sharing intimacies. I tell Jared his father asked me to speak with him because I happen to have a lot of personal experience with crack cocaine.

"I am not smoking *crack*!" Jared interjects vehemently. "I am *freebasing* cocaine. There's a big difference." There isn't. Nonetheless, I acknowledge the elevated social status of one of the most vicious drugs ever unleashed on mankind and concede I made an error.

Jared, after two decades of drug use, is no stranger to uninvited discussions regarding his "problem." Like me, he began with marijuana at around age eight, moved on to harder drugs and for the past five years has been the prisoner of a crack habit.

Earlier attempts at rehabilitation have failed and, as he sits there beside me leaning as far away from me as his chair and gravity will allow, his expression is almost haughty. I lie and say I don't have much time and will keep it brief. Once Jared realizes my purpose is not to wring an admission of wrong-doing out of him or to patronize him, he begins to relax. It also helps that I tell a pretty good story.

I tell him how easy it was for me to procure drugs, how much I enjoyed getting high, the feelings of invincibility, higher awareness, increased creativity, all the illusory and transitory "benefits" of the drugs. I also tell him about the crashing, the depression, the hopelessness, the fatigue and physical malaise, the pain of estrangement from my family that could only be alleviated by getting high again.

Finally, I tell him of the day I realized taking drugs was no longer a recreational activity but a necessity in order to function at all. I tell him about the long slow skid whereby each standard of integrity I once held was traded away, not just for another fix but for another day in which to avoid the reality of what I was doing and what I had become.

Occasionally Jared nods in agreement to our common experience. I politely override any attempt on his part to interject. This is not a confessional proceeding. Jared's rapt attention to my narrative reveals that he knows he's in the company of someone who knows the score. At one point I segue into a verbal, full-color description of the program.

An intervention is *always* a sales pitch, so pitch the program in a way to get the addict to buy.

I tell Jared about the rehab center, about the bunny rabbits, the birds, the space, the distance from his work and his family, the ocean air, the privacy, the grounds.

I tell him he would be free to leave at any time, *always a crucial selling point for someone who's entire existence is keyed to escape.*

Finally, I sit back and say, "Listen, your family has something they want to tell you. I told them to keep it brief and to not beat up on you. Otherwise," I add, "I'll be on my way."

"Fine." replies Jared, as he gets up from his chair. "Let's get this over with. I'll listen to whatever my family has to say, but I am not going to do this program." This last assertion is delivered with considerable temerity, despite the fact he's still in his bathrobe at 2:00 in the afternoon.

"Jared, no one is here to try to force you to do anything," I tell him. "Your family wants to tell you something. I suggested to them they write down what they want to say in letters which they will read. I'll take the blame for those. Each member of your family has a lot to say, so I asked them to keep it brief and concise and that's what they have promised to do."

He nods as if he is on a tight schedule and walks quickly back into the house.

Jared's sister Debbie will be arriving in Los Angeles later that evening. Earlier in the week, she and I had a rather animated discussion over the phone about denial which, in her view, is the entire reason for Jared's continued drug use.

The truth of the matter is that denial is simply a smokescreen of lies put forth by the addict for the benefit of people who may pose a threat to his freedom. *It is not a measure of the addict's actual awareness about his own problem*, and I make that clear to the families I work with.

Denial equals lies. It's that simple. Sure, part of the addict's thinking is the problem isn't as bad as it is. There is a loss of perspective because the addict is on the *inside* of the problem and can't see what others see. This does not mean, however, the addict needs to admit to anyone other than himself that he may need help. This is why I strongly advise families against trying to turn an intervention into a therapeutic process wherein the addict is pressured to reconcile with his past behavior in front of an audience, especially in front of his own family.

I had wanted help with my own addiction for years, yet I never went to my family. *I was more honest with my dealer than I was with my own mother.* Jared is more aware of the danger of his condition than anyone else can possibly be because he is living it.

The greatest obstacle to accepting treatment will be his pride, his desire to handle the situation on his own.

Winny and Cindy turn to look at Jared as he comes into the room, Richard stands, greets his son and motions for him to sit, smiling all the while. Jared chooses a deep, heavily padded leather chair opposite his father. I come inside and sit with the two women on the couch.

"Look," Jared says. "I want to make something very clear right from the start. *I am not smoking crack;* I am freebasing cocaine; there is a huge difference." (Not.) "I'm handling it. I'm taking care of it."

Jared looks at each of us, challenging us to refute this assertion. Each of us looks back at him with our own truths in mind.

Jared's mother Winny sees what he wants her to see: a successful, sought-after music video editor with celebrity connections and a big house in one of the most exclusive neighborhoods in Los Angeles. She sees her grown son, albeit unshaven and dressed in a bathrobe. But, after all, we had surprised him; he was not expecting us. In short, everything she sees is colored by her own good opinion of her son.

Jared's father sees his grown son—apparently sober, lucid and polite—in command of himself and a little put off at the intrusion into his home. He does not see any evidence of drug use: no lines of cocaine on the coffee table, no handguns, no bimbos, no addicts passed out anywhere in the living room. The house is relatively clean and presentable.

Cindy's view of her brother's condition is more critical and she tells him so, pointing out how pale he is, wondering aloud how long he has been knocking around the house in the bathrobe. She comments he looks vastly different, and not in a good way, from when she last saw him a few months earlier.

What I see is a human being in bad shape. Jared fidgets in his seat, nervously clasping and unclasping his hands. I see the neglect of a person that drug use engenders: the food stained bathrobe, the disheveled hair, the several day's growth of beard, the red-rimmed and restless eyes. The paranoia fed by a cocaine habit manifests in many ways, with evasiveness pervading every statement and attitude.

I cut into the nervous chatter before anyone can open a debate with Jared about going into treatment.

An intervention that devolves into a debate tends to be a losing battle. You cannot win an argument with an addict who is determined not to let you.

Cindy is primed to launch right into the subject. Heading her off, I ask her to read her letter to Jared.

Having Cindy read her letter first has another advantage. She and Jared have not spoken in some time and Jared is very curious about what Cindy has to say to him. As he listens to her, Jared is visibly moved. I always feel privileged to be a part of these meetings. Cindy's letter is loving, full of concern and frankly expressed.

Then his mother and father read their letters to him. Jared's general demeanor is one of indifference, as though he has heard it all before and nothing could or would have any effect on him. He maintains this attitude throughout the reading of the letters, repeating at the end of each one he isn't going to go to treatment. Jared is moved, even mollified, by his family's statements of love and concern, but no one seems to make a direct hit with him, even though each person has obviously given time and thought to the letters, which are all deeply sincere and loving.

When you get close to hitting home, the addict will often fight back or break down. Jared does neither. "I appreciate your taking the time to talk to me about this and to write these letters, but I really don't have a problem. I know what I'm doing, and I know how to control it. We've had these talks before, and the answer is the same. I'm doing fine. I don't know who's telling you I'm not doing fine. I love you all and thank you for coming, but I have work to do. Stay as long as you like. I'll be in my bedroom working on a video for one of my top clients. I have responsibilities and a deadline to meet." With that, Jared stands up and walks out of the room. We hear a door open and close and that's that.

Richard, Winny, and Cindy are all visibly shaken by Jared's response, but none of them thinks it was unexpected or unusual.

Overall I'm pleased with the meeting. I got to size Jared up a little bit. I got to see his modus operandi with his family, and theirs with him. I observed their reactions to him and their unquestioning acceptance of his viewpoint regarding his drug use.

Neither Richard nor Winny wants to believe their son is not in control of his life. They immediately accept his rejection of their offer of help. They cannot believe this sensitive, brilliantly creative man sitting before them is wandering dangerously close to an abyss.

Over the years, Jared's insistence that his family's attempts to help him were futile have always worked for him. The script is always the same. "I am in control of my life; you can't *make me* accept help."

Richard is now going full speed down this track. "He looks okay to me. He makes good money. He's famous in the music industry. He's accomplished more in his life than I had at his age. I don't see why we need to badger him about drugs when I don't even know what they're doing to him. I mean, really, he looks okay. I just don't like bothering him about it. He's a grown man, after all. So, he's always in his bathrobe. *So what?*"

Winny backs up her husband, "Look how clean his home is. Look how well he's doing professionally. I don't want to embarrass my own son by *nagging* him about drugs. It has never worked and it didn't work today. I love my son. I want him to do well, and I don't want him to hate me just because I don't like him to do drugs. I don't want to go through with this. If Jared says he can handle it, let him handle it. *Where is the problem?*"

Most families would probably have to think about this for a minute, but part of my job once I'm hired is to make sure even internal family arguments do not interfere with getting the addict to treatment. To a large extent, the mechanisms that shackle the family can help keep the addict right where he is.

What Richard and Winnie are telling us is they don't believe Jared is in bad enough condition to justify treatment, which implies there is no need for an intervention. So why have they hired me and flown the rest of the family in from across the country?

This isn't my first rodeo, so I decide to take the time to pick up the other daughter at the airport. If I'm lucky, she'll be my sounding board.

Debbie isn't hard to pick out. She bears a strong resemblance to both Jared and Cindy; a small build, medium height. light brown hair and dark brown eyes. She is dressed in a windbreaker, jeans and running shoes. Having been instructed to look for the man carrying a small brown dog, she walks right rapidly towards me, introduces herself and says, "Well, what do we do about this?" and keeps on walking.

I think to myself, "I'm going to like this one. We're going to get along just fine!"

Driving back to Jared's house, I carefully coach Debbie, who is by far the most outspoken and volatile in this outspoken and volatile family. Her role is key in that she and Jared had always been very close growing up. She's the least likely to buy into Jared's excuses for not handling his scene but, at the same time, she's the most likely to attack him on the subject. I don't want a detonation. I just need her to get her message across.

"All I want you to do is read your letter, observe his reaction, and ask him if he's willing to give the program a try. That's all." Debbie listens carefully and seems to understand what is needed. It's late. I drop her off at Jared's door and head home.

The family needs to carry this crucial step through to completion on their own. They've all been well-coached on the steps they need to take, and I can't be there in the middle of the night. If I am, Jared will assume this is all my doing and, even though it is, I need him to believe that it's all the family's doing. Otherwise, he'll just shoot me down and wait me out.

The next morning we're having breakfast at a pleasant little cafe on Hillhurst Avenue, and I learn that several things had happened the night before. Jared had apparently been free-basing while working on his video deadline and, when he emerged from his bedroom and found Cindy *and* Debbie sitting on his couch, his demonstrated euphoria didn't fool Debbie for a minute. She said she was struck immediately with how thin he was, how artificially gleeful he seemed, insisting that everything in his life was going exactly right. Neither Winny nor Cindy was aware Jared had done coke in his bedroom during their visit and wanted to know, "How do you tell when someone is on a drug?"

Like most people in the same situation, they couldn't see what was right in front of them. Debbie, however, said she could tell from his bloodshot, slightly wild eyes, the dilated pupils, the pallor of his skin, the wide grin, the deliberate movements and careful speech that Jared was "higher than the Almighty." He was also much more briskly rude with his family, and defensively assertive he did not need their help.

But none of this seems to be registering with anyone else, so I am sorry that Debbie will only be a staying a day. She could be quite an ally.

"He told me he already knew why I was there," she continues, "and he said it was all very thoughtful. He actually said it was 'impossibly warm and fuzzy' but a little bit insulting because he 'had everything under control.' He was sorry I had taken the time and expense to come to try to pressure him into solving a problem that is 'a complete non-issue.'"

Debbie pushes the uneaten portion of her breakfast around her plate with her fork as Cindy takes up the narrative.

Cindy describes Debbie's letter as *direct,* saying that she had read it slowly, looking at Jared often to make sure she had his attention. She told him *why* she loved him—just as I'd coached her to do—the reasons, the qualities he has, what she misses about him, things that are significant to him and to her. She reminded him of who he *can* be, that he can be himself again instead of a drug-fueled facsimile. Cindy tells us Debbie had read her letter through tears but never allowed her voice to break. She always engaged him, making sure he heard every word. "It was so quiet, I swear no one breathed. No one said a word. I watched Debbie and Jared. It was like no one else was in the room. Then at one point Jared started to struggle like he was holding something back, and then he cried too. At the very end, Debbie folded up the letter and looked at him and said very gently, 'Would you be willing to give the program a try?'"

And Jared said, "*Maybe* I will."

We all listen and, upon hearing about Jared's last statement, everyone lets out a sigh of relief.

I outline a plan to invite Jared to go with the family and *visit* the program. This will be the next step. His mom has a bag packed in the car full of all new clothes and toiletries in case we can get him to stay.

When Jared opens the door to us later that day, Helen Keller could see that he's stoned. Still in his bathrobe and smelling unwashed, Jared has added another day's growth to the hair on his face. His demeanor is distracted, his greeting falsely hearty and a little panicky. He has the clammy, shiny, gray skinned, jittery look of a guy who...well, who's been smoking crack for three days.

He invites us in and yells *"sh*t!"* loudly as he bangs his toe on the doorstep. Richard demurs and explains we're planning to go see the facility.

"Would you like to come with us?" asks Debbie.

"Oh no, no thanks, I have no interest in that. And I don't want to listen to any more letters either!" As he says this, Jared appears to swell up like a Bantam rooster, ready to deflect any attempt to coerce him to join the expedition.

"Okay, well we'll be back in little while." Debbie gives him a peck on the cheek.

I usher everyone into the car, and we speed off, leaving Jared gaping on the doorstep, one hand on the door knob and the other plunged into the pocket of his bathrobe.

I had coached the family about the dangers of believing interventions only take an afternoon or two. Sometimes they do–they certainly can, but it's folly to believe they will. That false belief sets families to think they have failed if the process takes longer. The fact is that, an intervention is doing whatever you need to do to get the person into treatment, *however* long it takes. If it takes a day–great, you got off easy. But if it takes a week, then take a week and appreciate the result if you're able to accomplish it. If the problem has existed for years, it may take some time to turn it around. If you are faced with the prospect of doing an intervention, then accepting this truth will afford you both peace of mind and a much greater chance of success.

Everyone in the family has seen the website for the program and has a vague idea about it, but visiting the facility, meeting the people there, and walking the grounds gives everyone a big boost in confidence about what they're asking Jared to do.

Seeing the facility for oneself can help immeasurably when the addict has a bad day and calls home making outrageous statements about being trapped in some stateside gulag, as a way of getting a family member to panic and pull him out.

Richard, Winny, Cindy and Debbie are much impressed with what they see. They meet staff and recovering addicts alike. They smell the ocean air, see the well-manicured grounds, the birds, the bunny rabbits. They are briefed on the program and the steps Jared will do to guard him against falling into the drug trap again. Cindy and Debbie chatter excitedly about everything they see and hear. Winny and Richard recover confidence in their purpose to help their son and, thankfully, Richard asks me to review the next step of the intervention. He shushes the women repeatedly as I coach them on what they need to do.

Jared could have, at any time, told his mother or father he was willing to go to rehab simply to get them off his back. His sister Debbie, however, had genuinely connected with him. Tears had flowed and Jared saying he would consider going is a good sign, a little bit of hope. But I'm not paid to be an optimist; I'm paid to be prepared. I assign Jared's statement its proper value. It is a good sign and nothing more.

Richard is visibly elated about Debbie's breakthrough with her brother.

He is certain that once Jared hears from them about how great the rehab center is, his *maybe* will become *yes!*

"How could he *not* go? The place is beautiful! He will have lots of freedom, *and...*" Richard exclaims, "*I'm* paying for it!"

We all need Richard's optimism. He will be footing a very hefty bill. If he loses faith in the proceedings, no other family member will be able to make it happen.

I don't want to dampen his enthusiasm, nor do I want him to misread the reality of the situation. Jared can, at any time, dig in his heels in an effort to dash his family's hopes.

"There's nothing wrong with hope," I tell Richard, "as long as we stick to the plan. I always hope for the best and plan for the worst. We have a plan and, if we don't need to follow every step of it, great. But if Jared starts to fight this, we are better off having a plan that covers all the possibilities, rather than ending up needing a plan we don't have."

"How serious is his addiction?" asks Cindy, "Can you tell how much he is taking? And is this stuff harming his mind?"

I can't answer any of her questions with real precision but, in my opinion, these details are largely irrelevant.

If you were to get an Oxford education on the subject of addiction and knew every detail in terms of exactly how much and what your loved one is taking or using, *it would not change the purpose or scope of your intervention,* which is to get the person on the road to recovery.

Knowing the chemical makeup of *meth* or how much the person is using or why, will not produce an intervention strategy. Knowing how much the addict uses or what he uses does to him does not alter the fact he is not in control of his life and needs to arrive in the program.

It's time to raise the stakes. I give Cindy careful instructions. She will speak to Jared alone and then leave immediately for the airport.

"Just before you say 'goodbye' to Jared, ask him if he is willing to go to the program and *at least give it a try*. He already told Debbie he might. If his answer is anything but 'yes,' tell him you can no longer make allowances for or overlook the hazards of the road he is traveling. Tell him very calmly that if he wishes to continue down this road he can, but you *also* have a choice to make. The next time you hear from Jared, it must be either to say he is going to treatment or to say he is there. Tell him that is the *only* communication you will be willing to have with him."

Cindy does not have any difficulty delivering this message. Jared reiterates he is not willing to commit to going to rehab, asserting once again he has his life under control. If he is upset by her intention to refuse communication from him, he isn't showing it. She kisses and hugs her brother and leaves for the airport.

Debbie, Whinny and Richard plan to leave Los Angeles Sunday night. Again, we meet for breakfast and go over the next step in the intervention which will be the most difficult, involving as it will the severance of all lines of communication between Jared and his parents and sisters.

This is not a matter of simply not sending a Christmas card.

This means no involvement in Jared's life *at all* and a complete withdrawal of support until he agrees to treatment and arrives at the program – a difficult task for any family.

The good news for me is the bonds of trust in this family are so great Richard even manages everyone's money. Jared is therefore completely dependent on his father for his investments, his bills, even his tax returns. As a successful and sought-after music video editor, Jared makes more than enough money to support his habit. The fact that Richard manages his money has, up to this point, saved Jared from the financial disaster that often results from drug addiction.

Richard initially will not agree to stop being Jared's financial agent; he says it would feel like abandonment. If, however, the money continues to roll in and Richard keeps handling Jared's obligations for him, Jared will never feel any real urgency to change. Ironically, by continuing to help Jared avoid financial ruin, Richard is indirectly helping fuel his habit.

Richard observes that Jared has blown through a lot of money in a very short period and, at one point, Jared even asked his dad to hide his money from him. He did this while pushing everyone away. It's almost as if he was holding up a sign saying, "Stop listening to what I am saying and look at what I am doing! Help me!"

Richard, a retired school teacher and a star athlete when he was younger, has no personal experience with drugs and is incapable of putting himself in his son's position. He cannot understand what Jared is going through. He does not understand that an addict sees the world much differently than non-users.

Richard sees Jared the way many non-addicts see addicts, as a reasonable person doing unreasonable things.

Richard resists me at first but eventually agrees to stop all communication, all financial management, all contact of any kind with Jared.

Family disconnection is a tactic, but it must *be real* to the addict, so *make it real.*

Later, I'm walking to the car with Debbie and Richard and ask, "How do you honestly feel about the disconnection?"

Richard answers he is fine with it, but Debbie challenges him directly, "Then why, when Steve is not around, do you keep telling Mom and me you won't do it?"

Richard is visibly embarrassed but plants his feet with an honest response, "I guess I'm just having a hard time seeing what everyone else is seeing."

Debbie rips into him, "How can you not see it? *It's right in front of you!*"

Her father reiterates his perspective, "I am just not sure the same way everyone else is sure."

I jump in, "Fair enough, but everyone else does see it, so do you want to err on the side of caution or do you want to err on the side of doing the same thing you have been doing? How's that working out for Jared?" I go on, "If you disregard my instruction, I'm not responsible for the outcome of this intervention. You are."

He doesn't expect that. He expects, since he's the one paying me, he can do whatever he wants to do and still hold me responsible for the outcome.

I soften my tone, "Look, Richard, I don't want Jared to be homeless. If it doesn't work, then go back to what you've been doing, what you're comfortable with. But right now, I need you to be okay with being a little uncomfortable." Richard is very thoughtful for a few minutes and then indicates his willingness to cooperate.

He and Winny go back into the house to inform Jared of their decision.

The report I get back later from Debbie is good, "Daddy went to Jared and said he would not manage Jared's money until he was willing to 'at least try' the program. Then Jared hands Mom a check from the IRS for a $15,000 refund. Mom takes it and says, 'We'll just take this home with us.' And so *Dad* says, 'What are you doing, Winny, put that down! It was great. It hit Jared right where he lives. He got *really* upset. I don't think he believed Dad would stop managing his money." Obviously, the disconnect is having quite an effect on Jared.

Thirty minutes after his parents say their goodbyes, Jared calls me and asks, "So what is this place anyway? What's going to happen if I go there?"

As an interventionist, hearing statements like this is significant. Jared is beginning to try to figure out *how* to be at the program or *if* he can be at the program, a significant change from being unwilling to go.

I answer his questions as Jared describes to me what took place with his mom and dad. He is still very upset. I tell him, "Look, your dad is upset, your family is upset. Just go down there, Dude. Stop thinking *only* about yourself. Do it for your dad. Give it a day or two. If you don't like it, freakin' leave."

"Fine." And then, "I'll go in a day…" but his voice lacks conviction.

The next day Jared finds out no one in his family will talk with him. They were now doing all the things they had told him they would do: the disconnection, the closing of door after door, leaving open the one door to a nice program.

I get a call later that night, and Jared tells me triumphantly he has cashed the check, "I'm high as a f**king kite! I'm cooking up a big pile of coke, Man, but listen, I do want to go. I can't stand that my father won't talk to me, he won't even take my calls! Can you tell my dad I'll go in a day or two??"

I tell him, "Look, I've got your back as long as you keep your word."

He replies, "It's a deal!"

Jared's parents and Cindy have already returned to their respective homes, but now another element is coming into play. Jared's housemate David is still in New York but plans to return to Los Angeles on Tuesday. I have already spoken to David, who has a 7-year-old son and is embroiled in a custody fight with his ex-wife who knows Jared has a coke habit and is now putting the screws to David over it. This makes David an ally-by-necessity.

I advise David that if Jared does not agree to sign into the rehab, he should consider a restraining order which would result in Jared's immediate eviction from their home and would be a much better legal position for David. By evicting Jared, David's ex-wife will not be able to use Jared to win their custody battle. David agrees. Besides, he's been living with Jared as a coke addict for years and is tired of it.

A restraining order would be an effective motivator but, unfortunately, Tuesday comes around and David has to stay in New York.

When I telephone on Wednesday, Jared is high again but assures me that he will be going in a day or two.

Richard is now *very* frustrated and, in some ways, begins to cave.

When I get on the phone with the family as a group, Debbie and Winny begin by ganging up on Richard. "You are e-mailing him! Can't you follow the plan for two f**king days?!"

Richard responds, "I'm hanging up."

I cut in. "We can't let the team break apart because Jared is the one who will pay the price."

Richard: "The team is not breaking apart."

Here is his only son taking one of the worst drugs he could possibly be taking. He's living in a condition Richard cannot even begin to understand. The net effect on him is a feeling of total powerlessness, and here I am telling him to disconnect.

Richard's heart *is* breaking, so we need to stay together and not let things tear us apart. I tell Debbie to stop yelling at her father and advise a softer approach.

I come up with another tack. Having seen Jared's incredible downward spiral considering what his father was doing, we can take this one step further and feign a health problem with the father. I place it on the table and, to my surprise, Richard is the first to agree.

"That's a great idea! Something reasonable, believable and not overwhelming to Jared. Tell him I am not sleeping or eating. Jared will worry himself right to the front door of the rehab center. He worries about the health of everyone in the family."

I'm impressed. Go, Dad!

We agree Debbie will make the call and Winny will back up the story should Jared call her. We are counting on Jared's extraordinary dependency on his father and concern for his father's health. I look at it as a 50/50 roll of the dice. Jared will go either way, so the ploy is worth it but must be well managed.

Debbie calls Jared and tells him his father is in the hospital. It has the effect we are hoping for. Almost immediately after the call is over, Jared is on the phone with me. "I'm ready to go. Please tell my dad I'm willing to go." Feigning ignorance of the situation, I ask Jared when to pick him up. "As soon as I can talk to my dad."

"Well," I say, "I don't know about that. I heard he was in the hospital."

"Are you lying to me?"

"Look, that's what your mother told me. If you think she'd lie, then there you go." We get off the phone.

An hour later, Richard calls. "I think we screwed the pooch. I wish Winny and Debbie would keep me in the loop. I just got a call from Jared and said I couldn't talk because I was in the middle of a tennis match! I had no idea they'd spoken with him." Christ.

Debbie is ready to kill Richard. Richard feels the same toward Debbie and Winny. My task is to keep the team together.

I speak with Debbie, trying to get her attention away from the failed ploy and onto the importance of staying calm.

An intervention is often little more than a controlled mess but that doesn't mean you have to become one. That's how families lose. It's important to keep that up front. Stay calm. Be willing to let go of the last plan and pick up a new one.

We need to regroup so we do, and we come up with a solution rather quickly. Come to find out, Richard often disregards his doctor's advice. So *now* the story is, he's just gotten out of the hospital and is playing tennis *despite* what he's been advised. Debbie calls Jared and plays the card. Jared buys it.

Once Jared decides, however, that his father is in no real danger, he begins again with his mantra of "I will go in a day or two."

I feel like the fisherman who loses his catch after reeling it halfway in.

Then that night something very dramatic occurs. Richard becomes apathetic. He says he doesn't care and no matter what we do, Jared is not going to go. He is so angry he leaves his house suddenly and without explanation in the middle of the night, exclaiming, "Jared will never go!" He leaves and he doesn't tell anyone where he's going. Winny calls and tells me. I immediately have her call Jared.

That gets Jared's attention.

Next, Debbie calls and tells Jared everyone is going crazy with worry, which in this case is true. Then I call Jared and leave this message on his answering machine: "Jared, good job! Your dad's gone and you're locked in your room smoking dope. Good f**king job. I hope your video works out." Then I hang up.

Such flourishes are risky, but the payoff can be worth it.

A few, tense minutes pass before Jared calls me back. His tone is entirely different now; he sounds quiet and concerned. He assures me he will be willing to "start the program in a day or two."

"What the f**k are you *talking* about," I say, right on top of him. "Your dad is *gone. It's the middle of the night.* No one knows where he is. All we know is he was extremely upset about *you* when he left."

[Silence]

"...tell my Mom I'll go in a day or two."

"*Jared*, I'm not telling your mom *anything* until you're in the car and on your way. For Christ's sake. If you're not willing to drop what you're doing for your own father and something happens to him! I sincerely hope you're ready to live with..."

Jared hangs up.

An hour passes before I get a text message asking me to pick him up the next day at 1:00 o'clock.

If the rest of us can maintain, the game is ostensibly over. There is no more play in the wheel. And, being at heart a sweet, caring and intelligent person, Jared chooses the road he knows he should take, as difficult as he feels that is.

Richard did return home in the wee hours of the morning, safe and unharmed, but thankfully this did not alter the course Jared had finally decided to take.

To my relief, the rest of the night is uneventful, and Jared is packed and waiting by his front door at the appointed time. Considering the amount of cocaine he has consumed that week he is presentable, but the evidence of his drug-induced psychosis shows in his wildly-darting eyes and his slightly hysterical laugh. He looks like he's been locked in a closet for two weeks, his skin gray and slightly shiny, but it's okay with me; he's getting into the car of his own accord.

"Come on, come on! Let's go!" he cackles. "I want to get started. It's the devil. It's the demon. It's that demon! You know what I'm talking about Steve!?"

"Yes Jared," I reply. "I do." And off we go.

Lessons from Jared

This is a good example of a family staying together even when individual family members were fumbling the ball, continuing to work as a team and, in the end, it paid off.

Jared's father shows us a couple of very important things. First, his indecision wasn't necessarily based on doubts about Jared's drug addiction, even though that's what he told everyone. It was the opposing fears of alienating his son *and* of not doing the right thing. We see the truth of this when Richard leaves his house in the middle of the night. In his heart, he is feeling an incredible amount of pain about what's happening to his son and helpless to do anything about it.

The effect Richard had on Jared shows us that you never know what's going to happen during an intervention or what you can possibly turn to your advantage. Things will happen you could never have expected but, if you stay calm and continuously regroup, plan, continue to plan and regroup, and don't let your team get separated, you *can* succeed.

Jared also shows us that simply because an addict has some money in the bank does not in any way mean that you are going to lose the fight against his addiction. Often, and this was the case with Jared, the addict will back himself into a real corner with his drug and alcohol use and become desperate for a way out.

The family and I approached Jared with respect even when we were directly confronted him on his drug use. This also paid off because in the end Jared was able to agree to go to the program without feeling as though he was losing face in doing do.

Afterword

Chances are you picked up this book because someone you love is addicted to drugs or alcohol and, even though you want him to get help, he has endless reasons not to accept it.

By the same token, one of the biggest problems families have when they start an intervention, is *they* find seemingly endless reasons *not* to do one...not *yet* anyway.

After the stories of successful interventions I have shared in this book, I'd like to share some other moments which I hope will help motivate you.

A woman called me one day to ask about getting help for her 18-year-old nephew who was experimenting with club drugs and painkillers he was buying at school. He was still maintaining his grades, so the family decided addressing his pill habit was not urgent. Two weeks later the woman called again to tell me his parents had found him on the floor in his room, dead from organ failure. *If they had not waited,* the outcome might have been much different.

A family in Texas called me and said they needed to do an intervention on a family member who was addicted to OxyContin. I urged them to take immediate action due to the severe nature of his addiction, but they had plans in place for Christmas and didn't want to lose their deposits they had made on their vacation rentals. Besides, they said, he'd been a drug addict for years, so what difference would waiting another month make?

In the end, the family didn't lose their deposits and they went on vacation, but after 20 years of his addictions, they did lose their son.

I talk a lot about what it means to do the right thing. We don't always know what the right thing is, but one thing is clear; the wrong thing to do is nothing. It's wrong to put off doing the right thing because of a family vacation, or because you simply don't want to do it yet, or because someone *else* doesn't want to do it.

There will always be a part of you that hopes if you just give things a little more time or if your addict can just swing that job interview he has this week, there is a chance, however remote, this will be the time he will pick himself up by the bootstraps, get some real traction, and begin to live way he should. But, at some point, you must come to terms with the possibility the part of you that is holding out is the same part of the gambler who sits at a blackjack table well past the time he should have departed, holding out in the hope his luck will change. The person you are trying to help thinks the same thing. I know this because I've been there. I believed if I could just get a job, or enroll in that school, or get enough money together to pay my rent, I would be able to pick myself up and move on.

All of this boils down to one simple fact. If you ignore history, it is destined to repeat itself over and over again.

Help *is* available to you. I'm just one professional in a large population of mental health professionals, interventionists, and intake counselors who devote their lives to helping families like yours. Take advantage of that. Most interventionists, myself included, do not charge for an initial phone consultation. Treatment programs will not charge you to take a tour. At the end of the day, whether there are pending court dates or illnesses or bad behavior or whatever is getting in your way, if you feel that you should help, then get *started*.

There will always be a litany of reasons to put it off. It's up to you to decide whether you're going to buy into that list of reasons to delay or, instead, pick up the phone, start moving forward, and put the addiction mess where it belongs, which is *behind you*.

"Every passing minute is another chance to turn it all around."

~ Sofia Serrano

Interventions ◆ Safe Arrivals

www.SteveBruno.com

Made in the USA
San Bernardino, CA
10 April 2017